Carlingford Lough

Text by Marie McStay

Paintings by Colum McEvoy

Cottage

Publications

First published by Cottage Publications,
an imprint of Laurel Cottage Ltd.
Donaghadee, N. Ireland 2004.
Copyrights Reserved.
© Illustrations by Colum McEvoy 2004.
© Text by Marie McStay 2004.
All rights reserved.
No part of this book may be reproduced or stored on any media
without the express written permission of the publishers.
Design & origination in Northern Ireland.
Printed & bound in Singapore.
ISBN 1 900935 41 4

Marie McStay

Marie McStay was born and educated in Newry and she now lives and works in Rostrevor. After studying for her degree at Queen's University, Belfast, she taught English in Spain before returning to teach in Newry.

As well as teaching, she works as a freelance Trainer and Life Coach – delivering Staff Development Programmes and other Workshops throughout Ireland. Occasionally, she works in Europe where she contributes to conferences and education projects on the subject of developing human potential for personal and professional enhancement.

Marie is a member of the team which contributes to the BBC Radio Ulster programme *Your Place and Mine*. The programme reflects life in communities across N. Ireland and Marie's is the voice of Newry and Mourne and Carlingford Lough area on the programme. She has also made documentaries of local interest for BBC Radio Ulster.

Colum McEvoy

Colum McEvoy was born and raised in Rostrevor, painting and drawing from a young age, and consolidating his knowledge by studying Textile Design in Belfast College of Art.

In 1979 he began exhibiting work in the Newry area and subsequently in numerous galleries in Dublin including The Hackett Gallery, The Solomon Gallery and The Board Fáilte Headquarters of the Irish Tourist Board.

His work is represented in many collections throughout the world and can be found in private collections in England, the United States, Australia, Greece, Spain, South Africa and Singapore. He has completed a commission for Allied Irish Banks in New York, was chosen by Guinness Diageo to exhibit his paintings on their promotional tour of Germany and in 1999 illustrated the song book by Colum Sands entitled *Between the Earth and the Sky*.

He currently resides in Ashbourne, Ireland, with his wife Deirdre and children Catherine and James.

Contents

Carlingford Lough

Carlingford Lough and the surrounding area is one of the most beautiful places on the east coast of Ireland. We have two capitals and three million people – Dublin to the south and Belfast to the north – within an hour's travelling distance; we are surrounded by hills, mountains, rivers, the British Isle's first summit canal, loughs and lakes, an economy which is once again enjoying a renaissance, a vibrant cultural life all within an area of approximately 48 square miles. But our visitors, or a journey away for some time, serve to remind us that here is a place of deeply rooted community around the stretch of water known as Carlingford Lough.

Land formation and mythology provide valuable insights into how we have developed as a region and a community. In the Carlingford Lough area we have evidence of settled living from Megalithic times but the origins of the landscape which shaped the lives of generations is found much further back in the mists of time – an almost unimaginable 350 million years ago when the area was deep underwater and great layers of sedimentary shale were laid down on the sea bed.

Today granite is the rock of this area. This is an igneous rock which was produced by slowly cooling magma deep beneath the earth's surface some 60 million years ago. Contrary to what may be suggested, this does not mean that volcanoes were active here. Overlying layers of sedimentary rock kept the rising magma thousands of feet beneath the surface where it gradually cooled and crystallised. Further igneous activity produced seams of hard rock in vertical walls leaving four of the structures known as ring dykes around the Carlingford Lough area – three behind the north facing coast and one in the Mournes.

Over a period of many millions of years the surface rock was eroded by ice, wind and rain to reveal the now solidified granite below, with the last ice age shaping much of the dra-

View from the Flagstaff

matic landscape we behold today. Travelling from the north and west, the glacial trail found the softer land less resistant to its pull. It dug into valleys and widened them. It deposited moraine and shale on mountain sides and shoreline leaving features like the Greencastle peninsula which offers one of the richest sites of these fertile deposits in the area.

At last, the estimated 2,000 feet thick ice retreated leaving in its wake a stand of hills to be worked over by other elements. It formed an inlet where it deposited its drift and boulder clay – Carlingford Lough – which received the water now making its way down two valleys meeting at Rostrevor. From the Newry direction, came a flow of water emanating from the northbound ice retreat which had filled Lough Neagh to its full capacity. To get to the sea, the water travelled along a path most of which would in later millennia be the route of the first summit level canal in the British Isles – through Portadown, Poyntzpass, Newry and Warrenpoint.

The ice also shifted boulders from one place to another and Clough Mór above Rostrevor is a fine, accessible example of one of these glacial erratics as they are called. Experts believed it must have travelled many miles before settling beside Carlingford Lough – a history almost as dramatic as the local legend of how it arrived there when the giant Finn McCool fought his enemy across the lough beneath.

That enemy was Benandoner from Scotland who challenged the mighty Finn to fight. Each set out to encounter the other. Their meeting point was Carlingford Lough – across the water they faced each other in contest. Finn McCool lifted a finger of stone from the top of the Carlingford Mountain and flung it across at Benandoner standing above Rostrevor. It landed at his feet but the contest was over because Benandoner was so frightened at this show of muscle that he fled back to Scotland. As legend has it, Finn McCool having survived many threats in his time, died on that very mountain top at the icy hands of Ruiscaire who laid him to rest. As he lies there, the rain clouds settle on the profile of his giant face to indicate the weather.

Whatever the cause, Carlingford Lough is surrounded by evidence of monumental happenings. Slieve Martin (485m), Slievemeen, Slieve Ban, Slieve Fada and Knockshee (346m) form the backdrop of hills behind the south facing coast of Carlingford Lough. The Carlingford mountains stand behind the north facing coastline of the lough – the highest is Slieve Foye at 586m and also visible is The Foxes Rock 384m. Black Mountain stands behind Omeath with Clermont Cairn at 510m and as the neck of the lough closes at Narrow Water, Castle Anglesey Mountain rises to 428m while Fathom Mountain sits at 249m overlooking Fathom Forest. These mountains and hills stand as testimony to the rigours of a long and lonely labour.

Clough Mór

It was into this landscape that early settlers, the hunters and fishermen in the Middle Stone Age, 8000–3500 years B.C. arrived. The waters of Carlingford Lough offered not only a very convenient means of travel but also an abundance of shellfish and other food.

These Megalithic people who settled in substantial numbers on the lower hillsides and around the Lough shores were builders and the stone in the region provided them with the material required to build their long (court) graves. They also left signs of their presence around Carlingford where 'kitchen middens' have been uncovered – remnants of rubbish pits full of oyster and mussel shells discarded after consumption in the first settlements of the region.

Neolithic people arrived next. Relics of those times have been found at Kilfeaghan and Ballyhatten where there are the remains of some of their tombs. The Kilfeaghan Dolmen – the cap stone of which is reckoned to weigh forty tons; the burial stone at Clontigora; a huge cairn at the top of Clermont and the portal dolmen at Proleek, Dundalk indicate the spread of Neolithic habitation as do worked flints found at Greencastle.

Stepping back into the realm of folklore and legend this is also the setting for one of the greatest of the Celtic Tales – The Tain. It was the time of Queen Medbh and a time when status was measured by the acquisition of animals. The currency of greatest value was the Bull. Queen Medbh – a profoundly competitive woman – taunted her husband at home in Roscommon about the wealth that she had brought to their marriage. He reminded her that having brought the White Bull to the relationship meant that it was he who had contributed more. And add further to her fire, she knew that this was a White Bull unmatched in strength throughout Ireland. There was no bull to touch him … except the Brown Bull of Cooley. Queen Medbh embarked on her mission to capture the Brown Bull. The Celtic War Spirit put fire in their bellies for they fended off the attacks of the enemy who had got wind of their approach. Onward they rode until Queen Medbh met the towering Cuchulainn, defender of Ulster and the Brown Bull. Cuchulainn initially proved himself to be the stronger combatant when he annihilated her advance guard. But his weakening strength opened the opportunity for the Connaught Queen to capture the Brown Bull of Cooley.

By this stage losses were so heavy on either side, that she and Cuchulainn made a pact: she would not advance on Ulster further if Cuchulainn entered a single battle with her bravest warriors. Deceitfully, Queen Medbh put a spell on all Ulstermen, weakening their ability to fight. But this had no effect on Cuchulainn as he was not a pure Ulsterman. And so he fought each one with characteristic valour. Queen Medbh, relentless in her selfish pursuit of power, underhandedly engaged Cuchulainn's foster brother Ferdia to fight the warrior.

This resulted in a three day one-to-one bloody battle which saw Cuchulainn survive to pursue the retreating Queen Medbh who had made off with the Brown Bull.

War ensued and the rumblings of the devastation reverberated throughout the land. Queen Medbh was reduced to pleading for her life from the warrior whom she had attempted to murder. In the final battle of this epoch, the Brown Bull of Cooley escaped and sought out its enemy, the White Bull of Connaught. In a battle reminiscent of Cuchulainn's three day one-to-one, the two Bulls raged and destroyed all around them. In defending Ulster, Brown Bull of Cooley was fatally wounded in victory.

This is a legend told throughout the Celtic World and that it was set here is a reminder that down through the ages this part of the densely populated east coast of Ireland has always been a focus of events affecting all Ireland and beyond.

In recent times, because of European and domestic political developments, unprecedented growth has brought renewed prosperity and optimism to this part of the world and with strong historical links to the USA and Canada, we find ourselves occupying a central seat in the international arena. This corridor is more than an economic run for flourishing businesses. Possibilities of collaboration across cultures and communities have once again been ignited, rekindling connections which lay dormant for many generations. Communities in and around Newry and Carlingford Lough tell the story of survival, renewal, decline and growth.

Throughout the history of Carlingford Lough, the villages, towns (and in recent times a city) have woven an identity as a place which occupies a borderland with considerable ease. The entire area straddles the border between north and south and is the meeting point of three counties. In previous times it was recognised as one of the more advantageous points of entry for invaders and freight carriers. It was also the point of departure for our ancestors during times of great hardship. Naturally then, we are accustomed to change. Living so closely to the Lough and having built the Canal to encourage trade, it seems we have developed as a community of adaptable people who manage circumstances with characteristic entrepreneurship. Welcomed or not, we have embraced the changes brought about through the vision of others for our region. Their motives may well have been self serving but without the labour and support of the settled people here, they could not have succeeded.

There is ample evidence from across the centuries to demonstrate the interdependency of the communities around the lough. Before Newry became a major port, Carlingford was the centre which received and dispatched goods. The pulse of economic life slowed down on one part of the Lough only to quicken elsewhere. Warrenpoint became the deep sea port for Newry, unable as the latter was to manage the bigger ships. Rostrevor provided the solace of peaceful surroundings for residents and visitors alike even before the trams from Warrenpoint carried tourists. Omeath offered a day out from Warrenpoint by a ten minute crossing on the Red Star – and creative activity in acquiring restricted goods during World War II! We have records of children from Omeath who once crossed the narrow stretch of water to attend a school built by Narcissis Batt at Clontifleece. The railway line linked Newry to Greenore and in the mid 20th Century, McGovern's Store in Monaghan Street, Newry carried goods to customers out as far as Greencastle in the area's first haulage lorry. There are many other examples of this interplay which provide the rich tapestry and colour of life lived through challenging circumstances for most of its inhabitants.

Farming is a strong feature in the way of life. Newry, being a Market town, was the meeting place of rural and urban life. Many families continue to have strong land links although in more recent times the issues of diversification and viability continue to present challenges. But the connectedness of one strand of life to another is very tangible in the experience of farm life around Carlingford Lough. Here we witness how the farmer used the sea. The harvesting of wrack – or sea weed – to fertilise the land was a very labour intensive task willingly undertaken because of convenience. Around an island that is not unusual, but in this area it was a strong tradition for the farmers of three counties to cooperate to feed the land from one shore line source. Another feature of

the partnerships which developed because of expediency and need, was the custom of bringing livestock from the nearby mountains which are exposed to severe winter weather, down to milder shoreline grazing until the spring has truly sprung in the hills. John Allen, born in Greencastle and now living in Warrenpoint, tells of the family tradition of bringing sheep belonging to his uncle, who lived in Attical, down to the fertile land at Greencastle during the early spring months in return for extra labour needed during the harvest time. Located in the narrow land between the mountains and sea, there is little choice but to work and live together.

Where we are on the map of Ireland appears to have contributed to our strong collective sense of individuality. No matter the location, you are never too far from a neighbouring county or jurisdiction. In Newry City, two northern counties meet, Co. Down and Co. Armagh. Co. Armagh sits next to Co. Louth on the road to Omeath which also has the invisible border between the north and the south of Ireland. Looking out from a boat in the middle of Carlingford Lough, however, there is no evidence of such divisions. The lines of division on political maps are a reflection of well documented struggles, but the landscape of lough, hills and mountains is home to generations who have farmed, fished and traded with each other and the rest of the world for a very long time. This is a unique feature of our community. When we look across the lough at the familiar scenery, few feel that it a different place. In Newry, we are regularly crossing boundary

Victoria Locks

lines – a day's shopping will take you from Co. Down to Co. Armagh and depending on the currency rate of exchange you may feel the need to travel the very short distance to shop in Co. Louth! The institutions, which down the centuries have assumed governance over our affairs, have been unable to undo the knot which binds us as people living together. Indeed, the position of being on the edge – of the Pale, the counties, the jurisdictions and the east coast has enhanced our inventiveness and tenacity. The distance around the lough, after all, is only about 43 miles by road and four miles at its widest across the lough from the salt marshes of Millbay to Carlingford. Paddy Small, a Newry man now living in the Tower House in Carlingford, talks of the regular jaunt by bicycle in the '40s and '50s from Newry to Omeath then on to Carlingford and then a nip across to Dundalk for the dance before returning down the Dublin Road into the town and home. And that was a weekly event.

Great leaders and events in all walks of life have emerged from this place. In commerce and trade, the arts and education, political and spiritual life, the Newry and Carlingford Lough region stands out as a significant contributor to national and international development and profile. It's proximity to the two main cities on the island of Ireland in current times, shields the fact that Newry was once bigger and more commercially significant than Belfast and that Carlingford was the major commercial centre north of Dublin.

From history names like St. Patrick, St. Bronagh, John Mitchel, Nicholas Bagenal, Major Ross, Bowes Lyon, Lord Russell, King John and Pearce are well documented as are their associations with Newry and Carlingford Lough. And, of course, there are many others. In times to come when we stand back to assess later contributions we will make reference to the key players in local industry, arts, politics, education, community development and sport. Indeed, the significant contribution they have made to increasing the visibility of this area on a wider stage is reflected in the naming of some public places and buildings to their memory. It was once said by Jonathan Swift of Newry citizens, but it is worth repeating and applying to all: 'Proud People' and … survivors.

Is there a family in the vicinity of Carlingford Lough which does not have relatives living overseas? Events in the history of Ireland provided exit cues for many. Too often it was severe hardship in trying to survive which compelled many to depart. In the 19th Century, it was the Famine which led to the exodus of that time. Until recent times, it was believed that Ulster was spared during The Famine. Although not the most devastated part of the country, it has to be acknowledged that many families from this area did suffer and seeing an opportunity to escape, they took it. Such plans were all the more accessible because Warrenpoint was a port of departure to America for the Famine Ships. Our historians are now beginning to reclaim some of that painful time. In the awakening

View from Arno's Vale, Rostrevor

consciousness as details of family members and tragic events emerge, we can trace a vast network of links principally into North America. There are pockets in the northern states which have a register of surnames which could only have come from South Down, South Armagh and North Louth.

In more recent times, the Troubles were responsible for the drain of people from their families and communities. Built on a peninsula, Carlingford and Omeath, although in the south, track their development more closely to happenings in Newry than to Dundalk. While the Troubles brought Newry and consequently the surrounding towns and villages, to its knees, from post World War II, the region around Carlingford Lough had already been slipping into decline. Poor politics and lack of investment demonstrated a lack of interest in the place by those appointed to manage it. Once again, economic survival meant leaving home and going to work in England. Families watched as their young people moved away to find a higher standard of living elsewhere. During the Troubles, many landmark buildings were destroyed. They were reminders of more prosperous economic times and represented a vision not shared by all. Newry, the main town, experienced decline, and young people coming from the town's surrounding areas to attend school, saw little reason to stay. During these times, the one imperative to those who could travel was 'Make a life for yourself somewhere else'. And many did.

Thirty years of the Troubles sent many overseas. Our antecedents experienced similar social, political and economic turmoil. And they managed to forge a life from their challenges. We are currently living through unprecedented change on many levels. The economic pulse is the first to be measured for health. In the 17th Century, Nicholas Bagenal first to 'own' land to either side of Carlingford Lough as well as Newry, had a vision for this whole area which resembles the activities of the 21st Century Newry and Carlingford Lough. Now we are getting close to the realisation of his plan to develop the Carlingford Lough area into a major, prosperous centre. When Queen Elizabeth I said 'No' to Bagenal and his ambitions, the idea was stored for only a few hundred years!

Visitors to and through Newry believe that the Mournes are directly attached to the City. When they stop and travel the short distance on either side of the Lough, as most locals do regularly, they enter a place which embraces diverse allegiances across counties, borders, living traditions with a history which tell stories of survival in the face of hardship. And if they stay into the evening and nightfall, the lights which recently have been moving further uphill with the development of housing behind Carlingford, Omeath, Newry, Warrenpoint and Rostrevor, they will see what we experience daily – a growing community which shares Carlingford Lough.

On the Water

When the first settlers arrived on these shores they were greeted not by the land we see today, but with dense impenetrable forests and bogland. So it was that from earliest times access to Ireland was obviously by sea. The inlets along the north and east coast were the gateways used and Carlingford Lough midway on the east coast seemed best placed for spreading influence north, south and west across Ireland. This was the waterway entry for Megalithic people onwards and it is thought that the Vikings, too, may have come into this part of Ireland via Carlingford Lough. Of all the factors involved in our development as a community of people it cannot be denied that this stretch of water has played the central part.

The Vikings

Lambay Island off Dublin housed the self sufficient monks who farmed, kept animals and crafted their own tools. Monastic life style was simple and rhythmic – working and praying and eating meat only on special days. The Vikings took the island and began their raids on Irish monasteries, murdering and stealing whatever treasures they could find. Raids were not restricted to monasteries alone because the rich farmland throughout the country was apparently fair game and battles were fought with resident Provincial Kings

for ownership. Competing tribes in their own land, the Viking gangs joined in raids to fight the Irish.

Another point of entry to Ireland was via Scotland across to Rathlin Island and subsequently into Ulster – the Norse form of 'The Place of the Men of Ulad'. Travelling along the waterways on the north coast, they gained access to the rest of countryside spread out before them with the promise of rich harvests. They were farmers and here – as in the rest of the country – they could survive using the skills from home. They travelled in long boats which were designed for narrow waterways, shallow and deep water. Another feature of the long boat was its flat bottom which gave them rapid landing ability and ensured rapid progress through Ulster. Down towards Armagh they travelled where they carried out a particularly vicious attack on the church and turned it into a pagan temple. A recent archaeological find in the banks of the Blackwater tend to confirm the Vikings presence and also add credence to the other version of how they came to be in the Carlingford Lough area. Many agree that by using the network of waterways they were able to access the Clanrye River and move downstream into the Lough.

Either of the above routes would undoubtedly have brought them into Carlingford Lough although the lack of archaeological evidence in Carlingford Lough of their presence there, adds mystery to the saga.

There is, however, a record of them having settled at Narrow Water which gave them easy access to the surrounding land and religious centres for example, at Killeavy. There must have been great fear in the area for the people had never before seen such boats and the religious communities which were the main targets for the raiders had until then been places of security. And moving at such a speed as to leave those on the shore-line shocked and running for their lives, these invaders come to take and destroy. The death toll was high. The frightening prospect facing the people of this area must have been deepened by the speed with which the Vikings moved in their long boats.

Evidence of the Vikings' invasion and methods of war against the locals is captured by Rostrevor writer, Siobhan O'Dubhain, in her moving story of *The Bell*. In this dramatic theatre work, the writer recalls the story of St. Bronagh, a holy woman at the time of St. Brigid, who came to the Carlingford Lough region and settled with her community of nuns at Rostrevor. Siobhan writes about the fate of St. Bronagh at the hands of the Vikings. St. Bronagh and her religious sisters had taken up residence in Kilbroney Valley where they became victims of the Viking war against religious communities. The Vikings came ashore and proceeded towards the valley to where the Bell of Bronagh sounded. That this was a community of women made no difference to the raiders:

Veiw from Clough Mór

But the holy house was pillaged
By a wandering Viking horde;
And they threatened blessed Bronagh
With the fire and with the sword.
But she chose immortal glory
With the saints of God on high
And the men who worshipped Odin
Heard the bell as Bronagh died.

From: *The Bell* by Siobhan O'Dhubhain.

Apparently, after their initial attacks in this area, as in many places the Vikings settled and lived at peace with the Irish. Carlingford and Strangford are the two places with names indicating Viking settlement along Ulster's eastern coast. And place names is all that we have because archaeological evidence has not yet been uncovered.

Once they settled down to share life with the natives, they married into families here. There is reason to believe that they felt comfortable in the area of Carlingford Lough. Its scenery of high mountains dropping into the water gives the place a distinctive sense of fjord. And for a while, peace and prosperity reigned. However, it was short lived for word of the prosperity in Carlingford Lough and Ulster had travelled, re-opening old tribal wounds. One of their historical enemies – another band of Vikings, sometimes referred in records as the Danes – came north to fight the Battle of Carlingford Lough. This, we are told, was a bloody battle fought on board the ships. The long ships would have been lined up side by side and combatants apparently fought hand to hand across them. Any wreckage or loss has never surfaced and the precise position of the Battle scene is also vague. One commentator believes that it is possible that the Battle took place just at the mouth of the Lough beyond the Bar – the high land below the surface, invisible to the eye but known to those who navigate the water. If that is the case, the treacherous rocks beneath the surface may still hold some evidence of the happenings 14 centuries ago. The Battle of Carlingford Lough is recorded as happening in 850 A.D..

The Vikings remained in Ireland until they were defeated in 1014 by Brian Boru at the major Battle of Clontarf. This one day battle engaged 20,000 men on each side and the Vikings ought to have won because of their superior weaponry. However, their lines were thin and easily broken up by Brian Boru, who died in the battle.

After this time, the area around Carlingford Lough grew out from Carlingford the town – strategically placed for the next part of the development of the region. And those who would go on to record events of the time were monks whose forefathers were themselves victims of the Vikings. Perhaps that is the reason history tends to view the Scandinavian influence as almost entirely malignant and sinister.

View from King John's Castle

View down the Lough from Rostrevor

CARLINGFORD LOUGH – BEAUTY AND LEISURE

Carlingford Lough was a busy place during the Middle Ages as marine traffic increased during the 14th, 15th and 16th centuries. The town of Carlingford was well placed to handle the trade coming into the country and on the east coast of Ireland it ranked in importance with Coleraine, Carrickfergus and Dundalk. Carlingford Lough offered a sheltered inlet from the Irish sea and once beyond the narrow mouth, trading ships found shelter along the north facing coast of the lough at Carlingford beneath the castle built by the Norman King, Hugh de Lacy.

Historically the entrance to the Lough was via the Hoskyn Channel, after Richard Hoskyn who designed the early 'Lough of Carlingford' Chart, 1857. Nowadays, boats enter by the Cut which is dredged periodically off Cranfield.

Carlingford Lough is 8 miles long. Positioned as it is between the Mourne Mountains and the dramatic mountains behind Carlingford town, it is easily identified from out at sea. Visiting sailing and cruising clubs are enthusiastically encouraged to call in to this 'the most picturesque inlet on the east coast.' Local people know the lough; visitors, however need to be aware of the potential dangers beneath the surface.

Beneath the surface of the mouth of the Lough lies a sub aqua thoroughfare of rocks, slopes and wrecks and along the length of this inlet, there are further threats from rocks which are scarcely exposed even by low tide. Depths in the Lough are greater than the immediate area beyond its mouth in the Irish sea. A usual sight for those living to the seaward end of the Lough, is a ship sitting out to sea waiting for the high tide. This ensures safety of entry through the restrictive mouth. Inside the Lough itself, depth readings indicate a dramatic fall from a relatively shallow 30 feet to a scary 100 feet. This plunge lasts for about a quarter of a mile and is situated between Killowen and Carlingford Marina.

Carlingford Lough is a continuum of the hills and mountains that surround it. It is not surprising therefore, that the charts' contour lines breathe in and out with more vigour in the bottom end of the Lough than toward the head of the Lough where the rising seabed levels out to the strand that Newry was founded upon.

Locals from Carlingford, Rostrevor, Killowen, Warrenpoint and Newry are the principal recreational users of the Lough. Killowen Outdoor Education Centre and the Carlingford Outdoor Education centres encourage the use of this rich resource. But visitors also sail in from England, Scotland, Wales and the Republic of Ireland in increasing numbers each year – once past the colony of seals on Blockhouse Island, they follow the transit line bringing them into Carlingford Lough with accompanying cormorants and herons.

View from Carlingford Harbour

When not taking part in one of the regular Sunday yacht races over the summer season between The Woodhouse at Rostrevor, Greenore and Warrenpoint, some of the boating community go fishing. Carlingford Lough holds a rich harvest for anglers and a world class record in June 2002 for a tope weighing 62 lbs is held by local man Joe Mulholland. The remarkable feature of this catch was that Joe hooked the tope on a 20 lb reel. With clever use of the clutch he was able to secure his place in record books. The Lough is considered Ireland's top tope fishing ground and it is only a matter time before the world's heaviest is hooked here.

The reason for the wealth in fish stocks is due to the wrecks which lie in and around the mouth of Carlingford Lough. Fish thrive undisturbed by passing marine traffic; dangerous rock formation and unrescued debris supply the environment necessary for proliferation and feeding and cod, ras, pollock and conger also swim in these waters in great numbers. Confirmation of the wealth of feeding beneath the surface can be further evidenced by the busy seabird life. Here we see constant high divers bombing into unsuspecting shoals or head down oystercatchers digging for juicy pickings. And the sea conditions allow for all year round activity. Except, of course, when the Carlingford Kettles are spouting.

A Carlingford Kettle is a most interesting feature to see – though very challenging to get caught in! And in all of Ireland, this is its only venue. Wind comes off the mountain behind Carlingford and Fathom and sweeps down on to the Lough. It travels at high speed and whips up the water's surface to form a spout at least, or a mini tornado at worst. It dances on the water, zigzagging randomly threatening to move all in its way. Spectacular as they are to watch from the shore – consider the sensation of one heading toward you as you windsurf. John O'Hare of Rostrevor saw one coming his way and, unable to surf away, found himself in the middle of it. For thirty seconds, it enclosed the windsurfer in a stillness and showered water down on him, before it moved sideways and off across the Lough. People talk about the particularly threatening 50 feet high Kettle which threw itself up into the air at the Marina in Carlingford a few years ago.

THE DARKER SIDE

While ships, carrying cargo from all over the world into this area in particular and Ulster in general, offered economic growth to the local community who could also partake of the Lough's benefits, there is a dark side to the story of the Lough, for it has claimed many lives in its time.

There is much agreement that this is a treacherous stretch of water. Locals will tell you about the currents which run on high tides; in fact, there are sizeable bodies of turbulent water which are clearly visible to the naked eye on the surface of the Lough.

Records of maritime incidents date back to 1824 with *The Barbara and Jeanette* in that year, *The Mary Stewart* 1838,

View from Killowen

The Margaret Ann 1892, *The Jason* 1878, *The Orissa* 1845, *The Frances* 1902 being just some of the many vessels which got into difficulty on Carlingford Lough.

Possibly the most infamous was the disaster which befell the *Connemara* on 3rd November, 1916. The *Connemara* was a mailsteamer and it was carrying over 80 passengers as she left Greenore for her usual crossing to Holyhead. As it happened, on board were a brother and sister who, earlier in the day at Edward Street Station in Newry, decided on the toss of a coin whether or not to go on the trip. The fall of the coin united them with others from this area in their tragic fate. As the ship entered a narrow stretch of water known as the Carlingford Cut near the lighthouse, she hit the Newry steamer the *SS Retriever*. The *SS Retriever* had been battling heavy seas since 4 o'clock that stormy morning. There is little doubt that the captain and crew would have been relieved at having survived the dark ordeal on the Irish Sea as they found themselves within sight of their destination when tragedy unexpectedly struck. With it's cargo of coal from Garston, the *SS Retriever* appears to have veered over to port and hit the *Connemara* at midships. Within fifteen minutes both ships had disappeared; over 90 people lost their lives. Local families mourned the loss of one, two or more members. To this day people talk about the tragedy, so deep was the wound in the community. They had embarked on what ought to have been a routine sailing, in conditions which had calmed after the storm and before reaching the open sea

channel they lost their lives. There was only one survivor, Warrenpoint man James Boyle.

If the speed with which these ships sank seems breathtaking, consider the equally appalling cruelty of the fate of 7 seven crew on board another Newry ship the *SS Alder*. In 1937 at the site of the wreck of the *Connemara* and *SS Retriever*, *SS Alder* was lying at anchor waiting to go up to Newry with a cargo of coal when she was hit midships by *The Lady Cavan*. Within 10 minutes the *SS Alder* had gone under with 7 crew.

Often referred to as Newry and Warrenpoint's *Titanic* is the story of the *Hanna*. Built in Maryport in 1826, the *Hanna* arrived in Warrenpoint in April 1849. This was during the Famine and the *Hanna* was destined to sail to Quebec on 3rd April with the Irish men, women and children who were hoping to find a new life in America and Canada. With optimism and the promise of new beginnings, she set out on her journey. But no news was heard of the *Hanna* until the end of the month when on 29th April a ship called the *Nicaragua* happened by chance to see a flag of distress on an ice floe in the Atlantic. Needless to say, the captain responded to the signal only to discover that several people in a very distressed state had been isolated in the ocean. The survivors were in very poor shape after having been left to their fate by the captain of the *Hanna*. According to their account, the ship had struck a reef of ice. The seriousness of the situation had

Cranfield Lighthouse

clearly robbed the Captain, Corry Shaw, of the cardinal rule known to all – that the captain is the last to leave the ship – for he called all the panic stricken passengers together, advised against over-reacting, told them to calm themselves, where upon he jumped into a lifeboat, rowed away and left them all to the consequences. On impact, the *Hanna's* bow had found itself sitting on the ice. This slowed down the action of sinking and gave some passengers the opportunity to escape. Sadly, and what must have been horrific for all to witness, was the crushing and drowning of about 40 of the *Hanna's* passengers. There is no evidence that action against the Captain was ever taken.

This story of neglectful cowardice is unique in the maritime history of this area. Exemplary courage was displayed exactly one year later by Captain McKevitt of the *Serifin* which found itself in exceptionally difficult conditions. In this case, with the ship in the process of being wrecked, the Captain had to be literally dragged of the sinking vessel. His courage is typical of the many testimonials which abound to the attention and care of the captains of the Newry ships taking passengers across the Atlantic continuing a tradition dating from the beginning of recorded time whereby people have entered and left Ireland by Carlingford Lough.

In the 19th Century, the major exodus of starving people facing unbearable hardship at home is very far removed from the arrogance displayed by the early invaders. But when we look at our surroundings we can appreciate the sorrow felt by those leaving and the excitement of those arriving. Nowadays, the larger boats on the water are trading amicably while the smaller craft are often locals who, from their exposed accommodation, perhaps come as close as is possible to appreciating Carlingford Lough as those first visitors would have seen it.

Along the North Shore

Leaving Newry to drive to Warrenpoint, the A2 road travels along one of the most beautiful routes in the area. From the busy commercial centre of a growing city, very quickly you are facing into the majestic Slieve Foy which stands on the Cooley Peninsula, immediately behind Carlingford. It appears to sit at the end of the dual carriageway. This, of course, is not the case. Roy Beattie, the civil engineer responsible for the design of the road, realised that with careful management of the route the traveller could experience a range of views in a short journey. The layout of the dual carriageway conceals and reveals details in the landscape – like the imposing Slieve Foy which is hidden for a while as the road curves into a tree lined straight stretch. Narrow Water Castle is revealed on the final descent into the town.

Either side of the route climbs into forest which is occasionally harvested leaving scars and bald patches on stony ground. The rapid growth of young pine ensures that this sight is short lived. But regardless of the harvesting, the proximity of deciduous trees in a calm autumn makes for a four and a half mile journey of spectacular colour and mixed tones. Forestry cottages, which have now passed into private ownership, stand directly opposite each other across this stretch of water. Locals believe that the forester looked out for the forest on the 'other side' since he had a much better view of his colleague's place of work than his own!

The landscape is a daily reminder of the inter-play between land and sea and, in the past, rail. The Canal at the Fathom Line and the Clanrye River with its banks of glar at low tide, converge between the two roads leaving Newry – one towards Warrenpoint and the other towards Omeath. A railway line once ran from the Dublin Bridge Station to Warrenpoint along what is now the bank between the dual carriageway and the waterway.

In springtime, Narrow Water Wood which runs back from the road on the left-hand side, displays an undercoat of bluebells, thought to be at least 100 years old, and is visible for several weeks before the trees begin their own response to growth.

As the road to Warrenpoint rises to its final point before the gentle descent to Narrow Water Keep, watch out for the evening cacophony of circling crows as, bound by the falling daylight, they make their way back to roost in the high reaches of the rookeries running along the foot of the land below Narrow Castle.

The final approach to the town of Warrenpoint, brings you to the gates of Narrow Water Castle standing directly opposite the original Narrow

Water Keep where the three counties of Louth, Armagh and Down meet in the water which lies beneath the Keep.

The Keep at Narrow Water goes back to Hugh de Lacy's time in the 13th Century when fortifications went up around the area to protect Newry further up the strand. Destroyed in the 1641 Rebellion, the Keep was rebuilt in 1663. An appropriate setting for romance and tragedy, there is a sad story attached to Narrow Water Tower and Bawn – the love-sick Lassara who dared answer her heart's desire against the wishes of her family and jumped to her death. Local poet, Michael Durkin, tells the story in his short ballad *Lassara's Leap*. A prisoner in the Tower, Lassara longed to be free to travel and see the world:

"...Daily she wept while nightly she prayed
That someone would come who would free her".

Predictably, her prayer was answered when a young Troubadour, regaling her with music and song, stole her heart. They fell in love but her family did not approve of this young man of lowly birth and so their love was crossed. The couple's destiny was entwined for they each died tragically – he by an arrow from the bow of the guard on the Keep and

Lassara was troubled and tossed in her sleep
She heard in a vision his voice from the deep
She raced to the parapet, sprang from the Keep

Narrow Water Keep

To her death and her lover who waited
Beyond forever, the currents they ride
The minstrel and she who dared be his bride
Their arms locked together they float side by side
They had found their own freedom together.

Michael Durkin

WARRENPOINT

Formerly 'Waring's Point', the town of Warrenpoint grew up under the Hall family at Narrow Water Castle. The first mention of Halls in Ireland was in 1603 when William Hall landed in Belfast with a group of Devonshire Men. In 1670, Sir Francis Hall – William's son, visited a friend at Poyntzpass and, travelling around, liked Narrow Water sufficiently to buy it from Joseph Deane. The large castle set back off the main road was built in the years between 1827 and 1847, and the some of the Hall family still live there.

In the early years of Warrenpoint around 1780, very few families lived here and they dealt mainly in fishing and labouring. Over the next two hundred years, its resident population grew to approximately 4,500. It is a fine example of a planned town – from the grid street layout with its large square; the proximity of the Park with it's bandstand to the Swimming Baths on the Promenade all adds to the purpose built feel.

In the early days of the small town, it was the arrival and departure point for seafarers going to and from Newcastle, Pennsylvania, New York and Quebec. In those days flax, which was needed for the linen industry along the River Bann, was difficult to grow. So, the Quaker families responsible for the linen trade sent their younger sons to America with the linen. They grew the flax there and returned with the flax in ships that had been built in Newry and Warrenpoint. Until the Famine really took hold, the main ballast was linen. But that was all set to change – the services offered by Warrenpoint were needed. Unfortunately, though, the ships were now to carry people.

For a long time Warrenpoint stood at the head of Carlingford Lough as a busy port in its own right as, unable to take the larger ships, Newry depended on the deep sea port of its smaller neighbour. Loading, unloading and transferring goods to Newry were welcome jobs – thus ensuring a vibrant and busy economic life. Being an emigration port, Warrenpoint experienced prosperous times during the Famine. People came from all over to travel away from Ireland and the stricken times. Coming to the point of departure required overnight accommodation and services. Thus, the seaside town began to sow the seeds of the trade it would later develop into tourism.

However, in 1850 the development of the shipping canal, Victoria Locks and Albert Basin, to facilitate the larger

Warrenpoint from Omeath

ships at Newry meant the loss of this activity and income to Warrenpoint. Emigration was in decline, too, and by 1852 there were only seven ships sailing out of Warrenpoint.

But during the years when the port was only handling the larger Newry destined ships, the townspeople responded with enterprise which would stand them in good stead. As the reputation of the beauty of the Carlingford Lough area had begun to spread, holidaymakers came in their droves to enjoy the sea air and the mountains. Those who had come over on ships from England returned with family and friends. From all parts of Ireland they travelled to Warrenpoint. Records for the late 19th Century indicate a winter population of 2,000 and a summer population of 6,000.

As in all places, the pendulum of prosperity swung back. Hardship and poverty gripped the town and surrounding area in the early 1880s because of the poor harvest on the farms. This impacted negatively on the tourism, trade and commercial life of the town. Not managing its own affairs – because of centrality at Newry – appeared to contribute substantially to this difficult situation. A public meeting at the Savings Bank, 1882 – where the Town Hall is now situated – voted by 118 for, 3 against (and 7 neutral) the motion that Warrenpoint conduct it's own affairs.

In 1899 the historic occasion of the inaugural meeting of Warrenpoint's first Town Councillors took place. There were twelve men at that meeting: 6 Nationalists and 6 Unionists. (The last meeting of Town Councillors took place in 1973).

Once again prosperity returned under the new arrangements which encouraged growth and instilled confidence. As a seaside destination for holidaymakers and daytrippers, Warrenpoint was in the business of tourism and entertainment and with the added value of splendid scenery it became a serious competitor to places like Bangor, Co. Down for the increasing numbers who were turning leisure into a regular event in their lives. Early 20th Century Warrenpoint was the place to be! And August was the month in which to book holidays. There were concerts – Percy French was very popular. Regular dances and military bands filled up the entertainments calendar. You could enjoy the Lough by taking a boat trip. If you preferred, you could spend time on the beach – hiring a bathing box to guard your belongings after having got changed. A seaside visit was not complete without the traditional Pierrots and in Warrenpoint daily shows were performed on a stage brought in via Greenore which had been erected opposite the Great Northern Hotel, which stood on the site of St. Joseph's Girls' Primary School.

During these early times, there was a pressing need to add to the town's facilities. The business case for more attractions was strong – trains were bringing hundreds of people to the coast. But not all of the swimmers wanted to jump into the sea.

Warrenpoint Docks

In 1906 consideration was given to the building of the Swimming Baths. And after some debate as to the nature and type of baths, agreement was reached and H & J Martin of Dublin were awarded the contract. The budget for the build was £4,750/4^d. The Swimming Baths enhanced the tourist trade and added a feature to the front shore which thereafter would become emblematic. This typical Victorian baths building was designed to be purely functional – sparse changing rooms and a swimming pool of sea water with the occasional jellyfish that a vigilant pool attendant would scoop out with a net. Ideal for the learner, it offered a shallow end but seemed to drop to substantial depths enjoyed only by the expert. This was where you learned to swim. Traditionally, those who grew up in Warrenpoint could swim from an early age – much to the envy of schoolfriends at second level in Newry. The focal point for outdoor summer socialising, Warrenpoint Baths appear in endless photographs – from the Victorian days of sepia when ladies in their afternoon walking gear took the sea air along the Promenade to current cyber images of the famous Sandy Bottom Swimmers who meet daily at high tide between April and September.

With all the high energy entertainment happening, a more reflective aspect to the town's culture was considered. A place of relative peace and quiet would balance amenities well. And so it was that the idea for a public park came to life. Captain Hall, who owned most of the land in Warrenpoint, leased the land between Prince's Street and Queen Street for the development of the park. The land was railed off and planted out. As with all matters of cost, the lowest price does not mean the acquisition of the most attractive design. This appears to have been the cause of some concern for the Chairman of Council at the time. Two designs were submitted for the design of the railings and gates. One – the more expensive – was submitted by Musgrave of Belfast and the other by Bayliss Jones. Chairman James Savage wanted the Park to be as attractive as possible and paid for the front gate and railings from the Musgrave design out of his own pocket at a cost of £89/14^s. The remainder of the railings, from the Bayliss Jones design cost £151.

The bandstand was added shortly after the park had been railed off and the planting bedded in. Once again, much debate took place as to the best position for such a feature. The current location was eventually decided upon and William McFarlain was awarded the contract at a cost of £222. The local contribution to the bandstand came from a builder called Carvill who received £27/10^s for constructing the base. Unique around Carlingford Lough, the bandstand was in use immediately. And down the years, it has been the venue for summer concerts in the park. Now managed by Newry and Mourne District Council, the gardens in the park continue to offer short respite from the street with their carefully managed lawns, borders and flowers. And the trees planted at the beginning of the 20th Century, have now matured to offer shelter and colour from changing seasons.

Warrenpoint Swimming Baths

And still in place is the town's crest on the bandstand – a seashell and two rabbits, placed there in 1907.

Warrenpoint boasted many hotels in its heyday. The Great Northern, The Crown, The Imperial, Harcourt's Temperance Hotel, The Victoria Hotel and The Ulster Hotel. There were many guesthouses, too, offering accommodation. During the War years, the town became a favourite destination for people from Belfast who came to take advantage of the proximity to the Republic. The Red Star, the Warrenpoint-Omeath ferry boat, carried lots of passengers going in search of restricted war time goods. Needless to say, there are many tales of the creative measures employed for the unlawful activities which predictably drew the interest of the local police. It is said that after the short trip to Omeath, people – particularly women – appeared to have gained substantial weight while out on their day trip. The appearance of a mother apparently in full term of pregnancy bemused some local police who knew the precise nature of the bulge. After all, when these passengers left earlier in the day, there was no sign of a baby at all. Not all officers, however, were prepared to turn a blind eye to the blatant smuggling. Even the most 'respectable' and religious people came ashore with meat, sugar and butter strapped to their bodies and covered with heavy coats.

By the '50s, the decline in tourism and visitors was felt in the town; this continued into the '60s. As with most other towns in the north, the Troubles in the late '60s and '70s threw any prospect of recovery to the wind. Unfortunately, the name of Warrenpoint is associated with one of the more atrocious acts of terrorism of that time. A bomb concealed in a trailer of hay at Narrow Water Castle on 15th August 1979 exploded as a lorry carrying British soldiers was travelling past on its way towards Newry. 18 were killed.

Today Warrenpoint is on record as being the fastest growing town in the North and the Square, which once hosted the Fair Day, is busy with cars and seasonal funfairs. Fast becoming a tradition is the annual International Blues on the Bay Music Festival which takes place during the last weekend of May. Once again, visitors come from England, Scotland, the USA and Europe to perform and be entertained. Predictably, they return with their friends. These echoes of previous times are in tune with a broader vision.

Festivals have become a feature of community celebration in recent times. In South Down, Warrenpoint holds its festivities in the week before its neighbouring small town of Rostrevor, just two miles away. Nowadays a twenty minute walk will take you out by the coast which was previously serviced by trams out to where Campbell's Garage currently stands at Rostrevor Dock. A piece of that tram track with surrounding cobble stones is still visible.

View from Arno's Vale

ROSTREVOR

As you travel toward Rostrevor village, the wide open lough view to the right becomes curtailed by the tree lined road. Four long-standing oaks in the square are witnesses to the colourful communities and changes over the centuries. Forested hillsides give this place a distinctive Alpine feel.

A strong feature of life in Rostrevor down through the centuries has been its association with spiritual exploration which predates Christian times.

However, St. Bronagh's story is the one which is often claimed to be the foundation of the village and continues to live in minds and hearts. In the 6th Century, St Bronagh and her community of nuns came to set up a place of sanctuary in Glen Seichis, as Kilbroney Valley was then known. From here, St. Bronagh and her community of nuns lived a life of prayer and good deeds. There is a belief that the sisters went to the shore to help sailors who had met with trouble at sea and nursed them back to recovery. Down through the years, the story of St. Bronagh has become woven into the tapestry of the folklore of the area. Evidence of her presence is scarce. An ivy covered wall in Kilbroney Graveyard is reputedly part of her original church. And it is claimed that many have had heard the sound of a bell … St. Bronagh's Bell. The story goes that hearing it was a bad omen; it was the precursor to bad news. The sound emanated from Kilbroney Valley – specifically from the area where her church once stood. But no bell was to be found. On stormy nights it could be heard and locals waited for bad news. It became known as St. Bronagh's Bell – after all, they said, she looked after those in need and this was her way of communicating. Many sceptical people dismissed the story of the bell – how could a bell toll if there was no bell? Well, confirmation of its existence was revealed in the early part of the 20th Century when workmen uncovered a bell in the trunk of an ivy covered tree which they were pruning. It was situated near the site of St. Bronagh's Church and this led to the belief that it was St. Bronagh's Bell. Having now found the source of the ringing, many interpreted this as proof, also, of the fact that St. Bronagh did indeed communicate forewarnings of tragedy to locals. The veracity of this part of the story remains to be proven. The Bell is now in the Star of the Sea Catholic Church and right into the 1980s its low tone was sounded during daily Masses – struck by the serving altar boy as part of the service, of course!

The religious and spiritual life of the village continued to occupy a prominent place locally and internationally. Early on in the Troubles of 1969, The Christian Renewal Centre on the Shore Road became established as a place to facilitate a deeper understanding of faith between communities within Ireland and beyond. In 1974, the doors of the Centre opened on the Shore Road to people from all Christian denominations to gather and learn more about each other and their common faith.

In 1997, the arrival of five Benedictine Monks from France appears to confirm further the spiritual energy of the place. Answering the call to create a place 'where all shall be one', they lived temporarily at Our Lady of the Apostle's Convent at the former Rostrevor House – or Topseyturvey House as it is called locally because of the mix of architectural styles added on over the years since it was first built by the Ross Family. The Benedictine Monks now reside in their own monastery in Kilbroney Valley – the valley of the Church of St. Bronagh. The monastery was the first to be built in the 21st Century and perhaps more remarkably, the first Benedictine Monastery to be built in Ireland since the Reformation. Many believe that the siting of this 21st Century monastery is no coincidence. The monks did not choose the land – it was given as a gift by a local man. There is an interesting detail in the design of Holy Cross Monastery built in 2003 on the Hilltown Road. The roof is supported by 12 wooden pillars, a feature designed to reflect the ring of trees standing in a field across the valley. It is said to honour our pre-Christian expression of spirituality. Once again, a bell rings out from the monastery across the fields in that valley to mark out prayer time in a day of work and study, a 21st Century echo of earlier times.

How the village got the name 'Rostrevor' is often in dispute. A commonly held view is that the Ross and Trevor families somehow amalgamated their surnames. In fact, the Ross Family arrived 100 years after the Trevor Family had left its mark on the village.

In 1610 an army man of a Welsh border family was stationed at Newry. His name was Edward Trevor and for a few years he lived at Narrow Water Castle. His first wife having died, he married the daughter of the Archbishop Usher of Armagh who was called Rose. He bought land in the area and set up a new house in 1612. He was an MP by this time and 1613 is the first recorded entry in parliamentary documents with reference to 'Ros-Trevor'. 'Ros' in gaelige means a promontory or headland, and, being a coastal settlement led some to believe this is how the village got its name. It is a also a short sounding vowel in Welsh. Hence, the confusion about the naming of the village called after the second wife of Edward Trevor.

One hundred years later, the Ross family arrived to contribute their part to the history of the village. The commissioner for Ulster under James I (1603 – 1625) was Sir David Ross and in 1712, his descendant, Robert Ross, built the house known as the Lodge which stood in what is now known as Kilbroney Park. In 1740, Robert Ross became Lord Mayor of Dublin and the property was passed to Sir David Ross, father of the famous Major General Robert Ross of Bladensburg. The Lodge was situated on the rise overlooking the lower meadow but unfortunately there is no evidence remaining of the house which was demolished when the estate was bought over by Newry and Mourne District Council and named Kilbroney Park.

On a rise above the road to the right-hand side coming into the village from Warrenpoint stands The Ross Monument. William Morrison, a Dublin architect, was commissioned to design and build the obelisk to the memory of Major Ross of Bladensburg who was a key figure in the War in America. He had also fought in Egypt and Europe but it was his role in the American War which has most significance for Rostrevor. He is best remembered for his leadership in the attack on Washington in 1812 –1813. Although considered unlikely, the capital was captured by Ross and his men. It appears that President Madison anticipated an easy victory over the first

and only foreign invaders. Dolly, the President's wife, had a celebratory dinner prepared – so confident were they of success. The dinner table had been set in the President's dining room and they were getting ready to eat when the unexpected happened. President and staff had to flee as Ross's men approached. In the panic to escape, Dolly with an eye to posterity, grabbed an image of George Washington off the wall. In keeping with the methods of war, Ross attempted to burn down the President's residence. But the building was not completely responsive to the arson attempt and within a few days the charred residence was painted white by the foreign victors. The Presidential Home in the USA has since been referred to as The White House. It should also be noted that Ross and some of his men enjoyed the food and surroundings of the residence for a short time. Securing victory provided instant notoriety for the Rostrevor man. But he did not live long to enjoy the glory. Ross was shot in a skirmish in a wooded area at Dundalk, USA. The irony is not lost on people from the east coast of Ireland! The Ross Monument stands on the site which had been identified as a suitable dwelling place for the returning Major General.

Rostrevor and its near neighbouring village of Killowen became household names in Ireland and beyond in the latter half of the 19th Century due to the exploits of another military man. The Four Courts in Dublin was the scene of the notorious court case between the Yelvertons – Theresa and Major William Charles. According to the story as it is now

The Ross Memorial

told, Maria Theresa Longworth fell in love with the disarming military man. She was a young vulnerable woman travelling home on a steam packet from France to England when they first met. Apparently, his plans for her fell short of the moral standards she valued. He was, by all accounts, a man who was charming, deceitful, manipulative and in financial difficulties. Whether or not he loved Theresa has never been clarified but what we do know is that he tricked her into marriage. Theresa deflected his amorous advances over the ensuing months, vowing to wait until they were married – which presented Yelverton with a dilemma. His intent was so determined that he charmed her into a questionable arrangement … a decidedly illicit marriage. But despite her apparent vulnerability – she was a young woman from a broken and unhappy home sent to France to a convent at a young age – she was equally fixed in her determination to have a proper church marriage.

He waited. Their journeys to be with each other saw them travel as far away as Tunisia. This was because of his military duties and postings and she took up disguises to be near him.

Eventually, their journeys took them to Ireland via Scotland – still unmarried, but each for their own reasons wanting to be so. And so, they arrived in Newry where they stayed at Dransfield's Hotel, Hill Street in Newry (where the Ulster Bank now stands). From there they travelled to Rostrevor to stay at Sangster's Hotel – now Sangster's Court in the village

square. Destiny awaited. The beauty of the place enhanced their passion; they fell in love with the coastal village which Theresa thought to be even more beautiful than Italy. And more importantly, she found a priest, Fr. Brendan Mooney, who was willing to marry them.

Father Mooney was reluctant initially to perform the marriage ceremony. It would seem that he was not convinced of the sincerity of the other party but Theresa, who had gone to see him surreptitiously, convinced him otherwise. After much mental anguish – had the priest ever had to deal with issues such as these before: She was Catholic, but was Yelverton? They had been 'married' before so could they remarry? Eventually, after deliberation of the situation, Fr. Mooney agreed and on 15th August 1857 they were to be married at Killowen Roman Catholic church – where the school is now situated.

But Yelverton didn't want any witnesses to this marriage. So, on that day they went by boat from Rostrevor to Killowen, Yelverton used delaying tactics and so they arrived at the church late. Mass was over and everyone had gone home, and the agitated Fr. Mooney hurriedly conducted the ceremony. At last, they were married. They spent three more blissfully happy days in Rostrevor staying at Sangster's and enjoying Carlingford Lough.

But before long, Yelverton was distancing himself from

her – leaving her isolated both physically and emotionally. His duties took him to foreign places; but more significantly he was denying her existence for he told none of his family about her, her miscarriages and her ensuing illnesses. The truth of her dire situation dawned on Theresa and she realised that he had deserted her. She contacted Fr. Mooney to get the marriage certificate which indicated a perfectly legal and holy marriage "the witnesses being Richard Sloane and Elizabeth Brennan". The next episode involved contesting the validity of their marriage in court.

The court proceedings demonstrated just how formidable a woman Theresa was. She handled the challenges put to her by the Rt. Honourable Abraham Brewster QC appearing for Yelverton with dignified and sharp insight. During the lengthy hearings, apparently, Dublin was full of the news of the unfolding story which made regular reference to Rostrevor and Killowen. Inside the Four Courts on the Quays, people gathered daily in order not to miss any instalments and were, it is said, moved to hiss, cheer and applaud as the details of the complicated arrangements between the erstwhile lovers swung between truth and deceit. But Theresa triumphed and won.

A protracted series of appeals, however, eventually saw the overturning of the Dublin Court findings by the House of Lords.

She went on to live a full life – full of adventure and travel. But, did she ever leave her beloved Rostrevor? From the 1950s, the family of the artist Colum McEvoy, lived in one the houses which were formerly Sangster's Hotel. They were aware of a lady walking the up the first floor corridor at night and disappearing at the turn of the stairs. Family members – including the artist – saw her spirit as it passed them. Was this Theresa returning to the place where she lived blissfully happy immediately after her wedding to Yelverton?

The Lodge which overlooked the lower meadow in Kilbroney Park, stood in the estate belonging to the Honourable Canning, second cousin to George Canning, Prime Minister. On his death, the estate was left to Major Lyon, who subsequently bequeathed the property to his daughter – Marian Lyon, the Queen Mother's cousin. This brought Royal blood directly into the coastal village and it would seem that she greatly enjoyed her time in Rostrevor for she is fondly remembered by some as 'a fine, erect, aristocratic woman who loved animals' who regularly walked her many dogs through the village.

Her interest in animals is recorded in rare photographs of yak which could be seen grazing in the meadow. According to older residents of Rostrevor, orders were given to shoot at anyone who tried to get into the meadow and the groundsmen regularly discharged pellets at youngsters trying to get a closer look. She kept horses – indeed she gave a gift of an

Arab Horse to a local man – and rare breeds of fowl were to be seen over the wall of the Fairy Glen.

Local man, Brendan McCartan was employed as her chauffeur and he tells the story told about the day she was travelling to Newry when she came upon a family of travellers along the side of the road. She apparently asked the driver to stop and she got out. To see if the travellers were safe and well? No. To check that they were looking after their horses.

Visitors today to Kilbroney Park enjoy a vast area of open space which owes a lot of its attraction to ornamental trees which were planted on the Canning Estate. The Pleasure Gardens behind where the Lodge stood, is a 'cathedral of trees', as local artist Jim Sherry once remarked. Specimens were planted having been brought in from other countries and the climate on this south facing coast supported their growth. Throughout Kilbroney Park, walkers can enjoy the rare Greater Butterfly Orchids and common Spotted Orchids found there. The Fairy Glen is the gateway to many forest walks, some of which lead to the heights of Clough Mór and Slieve Martin.

THE FAIRY GLEN

For many visitors the Fairy Glen is Rostrevor and the view into it from the gate – which was once locked to locals by the inhabitants of the Canning Estate but then re-opened under protest – is one favoured by artists. The ivy cottages to the left sit at the foot of Water Street, once the main street in the village. Water Street forded the Glen River, turned right to connect to the main road to Greencastle and left to run up to Newtown.

This was once the thoroughfare to Newtown and is still used daily by villagers. But in years gone by, builders walked to the spade factory which was in the process of being erected when World War I broke out. The men's presence was needed on the battlefields and the factory was never completed. The unfinished brick building still stands a few yards through the Forestbrook entrance to the Fairy Glen on the right.

The Fairy Glen – so named because of the belief that Brooneys or 'bad fairies' lived there and had powers to trick passer-by – takes the walker towards Ross's Planting which lies just ahead of The Salmon Leap. The river below will let you know how much water is on the mountain. There are days, when after torrential rain has fallen, the flood rushing down to the sea swells beyond the banks and the noise of it is as spectacular as its tangible high energy. When it is sober, pools of still water appear to ripple just below the surface with the dart of tiny trout and the riverbed is clearly visible. Over the years, pollution reduced the fish stock to nil, but recently local fishermen have reported an increase – including salmon – and the introduction of groins along the Glen River by the local fishing club is an attempt to help restore the river's harvest.

The Fairy Glen, Rostrevor

The Fairy Glen has always been of particular interest to environmentalists and conservationists because of the wealth of indigenous and visiting wildlife. The Kilbroney Conservation Centre runs down to the Glen River from the back of the Church of Ireland Vicarage on the Kilbroney Road.

KILLOWEN

Killowen is the district a short distance from Rostrevor. This is the place where the Yelvertons were married. The little church is now the school and is on the Old Killowen Road. The small village of Killowen sits on the shore and from the Lough, the hills behind look as though they drop directly into the water. Although locals now have to travel into Rostrevor to the nearest shop, Killowen was once well served for its needs. Five shops and a post office kept business local and helped to maintain this community which also farmed and fished. It was along Killowen shores that wrack was traditionally harvested.

Wrack is seaweed harvested for its fertilising qualities. It contained highly valued nutrients and farmers who applied themselves to this labour intensive harvesting every springtime earned much needed income. Mark Brennan, of Kilfeaghan, talks about his older relatives reporting up to 'about one hundred carts' on the shore gathering wrack. It is a long time since there was wrack harvesting but the outline of the wrack beds is still visible.

Killowen's name has become known far beyond the Carlingford Lough area because of two or three particularly well-known people. We have already seen how the Yelvertons contributed to the exposure of a slice of the coastline. But there are others.

At the time of his death it was thought that the tallest man in the world came from Killowen. Born to James Murphy and Peggy nee Cunningham on 15th June 1834, he was christened Patrick. Patrick grew up with his family in Kilfeaghan and there was no evidence in his early life that things would turn out quite as they did for him. When he arrived at the age when growth is expected to stop, Patrick kept growing. And his growth continued until he arrived at 8 feet and 1 inch high. Many stories have been handed down about Patrick – apparently he was to be seen lighting his cigarette from the gas street light in Rostrevor! – but more interestingly, concrete evidence of his height is to be found at the foot of Kilfeighan. A house was being erected there and the builders invited him to stand against the gable where they marked his height in stone. Although covered in ivy, the mark remains to this day.

News of Patrick Murphy travelled. On one occasion, an invitation came from Dublin Corporation. Patrick accepted

View from Kilfeaghan

the invitation but refused the appearance fee. He felt that if the people of Dublin wanted to see a fellow Irishman, they ought not to have to pay for the privilege. Off he went and walked around the streets of the capital to let them see the Giant Murphy from Killowen. But closer to home, he was noted for the unique way he had of sorting out troublesome individuals. It is said that when his patience ran short with someone or other he would lift them off the ground and put them over the nearest hedge. On one occasion, he stepped in to sort out inappropriate behaviour between two footballers by lifting them off the ground and knocking their heads together.

One career route for Patrick was the circus. He joined a travelling circus and there is a publicity photograph of him in Henry Kavangh's pub in the square, Rostrevor. Unfortunately, Patrick fell victim to smallpox while in France and died at Marseilles on 18th April 1862. His remains were embalmed and returned to Killowen for burial. You will find his grave with an inscribed monument in Kilbroney Graveyard, Rostrevor. It reads:

Of your charity pray for the soul of
PATRICK MURPHY, KILLOWEN

(The Irish Giant)
To whose memory this monument has been erected
By a few friends and admirers.
R.I.P.

Another man of note to come from this area was Lord Charles Russell of Killowen. Although born in Newry in 1834, Lord Russell spent most of his childhood in Killowen – specifically at Seafield House. His upbringing was strict and there was much emphasis on the importance of education and learning. But the concentration required by such application was relieved by the great outdoors. Living where he did, Killowen offered the full spectrum of activities available then on water and up mountains.

When Charles' father died in 1845, the family moved back to Newry. From here, Charles continued his education and the rewards of that endeavour were to bring him to the highest position in his chosen profession. After studying at Belfast and St. Vincent's Castleknock, Dublin he went on to be articled before practising as a solicitor with a Belfast firm. It was not long before he decided to go to England where his reputation as a leader in his field spread and his wealth increased annually until, as records show, his earnings in 1886 were £20,000.

A man of such professionalism and enjoying a high profile within the right circles was surely destined to continue climbing. His early life experience – combining as it did hard work at the books and scaling the hillsides for relief and pleasure – appears to have been something of a template for later events. In 1894 he became Attorney General and was appointed a Lord of Appeal. Within one month, he had risen to the position of Lord Chief Justice of England – a rare event for a Catholic in those times. His reputation spread far beyond Ireland and Britain and mirrored the warm affection those at home had for this lawyer, judge and formidable parliamentarian.

A little earlier (in the 1770s) the Pollocks of Newry had built a two storey house on the site which was to become home to Ballyedmond Castle. Built of granite, the house was significant because the United Irishman William Drennan visited it often. Other visitors to the house included the author Maria Edgeworth and Lady Emma Hamilton.

Alexander Stewart was an aide-de-camp to the Duke of Wellington and in the 1830s he came to Killowen. He owned the land that this house had been built on and during the Famine, in 1849, he built the Castle. The Castle was constructed using specially imported red brick from Wales and it is of Dutch design. An interesting feature of the grounds is that many rare and specimen trees were planted in the formation of the Battle of Waterloo.

Ballyedmond Castle passed to several owners over its short history. Notable of these was the Nugent Family. It was they who left the 'many specimen big game trophies – mainly shot in India by the late Major Arthur Nugent' according to promotional literature from the times when it was a hotel in the '50s and '60s. The Nugent Family lived at the Castle during the first half of the 20th Century and experienced some sad and troubled times there: it was raided for fire arms during the first Troubles of 1919-1922, the American Soldiers arrived there during World War II and there was the tragic death of one of Major Nugent's daughters.

In the second half of the 20th Century it became a hotel. At that time, it was described as standing 'on 28 acres of parkland and terraced gardens – overlooking Carlingford Lough, and is one of the most beautifully situated Hotels in Ireland'. It offered Guests the opportunity to take part in sporting activities such as golfing, boating, swimming and pony trekking. The Bill of Fare from the early '60s indicates:

Bed and Breakfast …..£3.25 per person
Three Days or more ….£6.00 per day

Plus 10% vat
Week-end Terms:

(Friday Dinner to Sunday Lunch,
including Saturday Dinner Dance)

JUNE TO SEPTEMBER …….£11.00 per person
OCTOBER TO MAY………..£9.00 per person
Plus 10% vat

As with many other parts of Northern Ireland, the Troubles

which began in the late '60s severely restricted the movement of people – especially for socialising, and Ballyedmond Castle Hotel became a victim. Business dwindled and the firebombs which devastated premises throughout the country, left their mark on the Castle. In the '80s it passed into private owner-ship to be restored as a country residence, and the original Battle of Waterloo feature has been revived.

GREENCASTLE AND CRANFIELD

Staying at Ballyedmond Castle was prohibitive for most, but not too far along the coast alternative accommodation was and continues to be available to travellers. The mouth of Carlingford Lough has beaches of sand and is very popular for caravanning and camping.

This is lowland, south-facing and is the departure out to the Irish sea. Standing on the beach at low tide at Greencastle and the crossing to Greenore appears to be but a short swim away. But locals will advise against it. They know only too well from experience and observation of swirling tides that to enter the water on this corner of the Lough is to risk life. Here you learn that the power of the element is mightier than the human.

Greencastle and Cranfield are tucked away off the main Newry-Kilkeel road. This was part of the gift to Bagenal as a reward for services to the Crown in the 16th and 17th centuries. Documentation from that time – 1611 – outlines the precise detail of the land gift:

> "…the Lordship of Greencastle and that of Mourne, with Haulbowline and Great Island … the ferry between Carlingford and Killowen, and the custom of herrings, commonly called the Herring Mease."
>
> (from 'Newriensis' Historical Sketch of Newry, 1876)

In keeping with the custom of the market culture which the Bagenals were keen to revive, Greencastle established an annual market and a Lammas Fair.

The obvious dwelling place was the Castle itself. The stra-tegic importance of its position requires little explanation. Stand in the castle grounds and there can be no doubt in the 21st Century mind as to the suitability of this rise as a build-ing site. The remaining ruins of the Castle stand today for visitors and it is believed that it was left in its current dilapi-dated condition by the Cromwellian army in 1652.

But Greencastle is unique for other reasons. The village hugs a bend on the shoreline. It has both a north and a south facing beach. From the north facing beach, the full landscape of the high and low Mournes stands before you. The mountains have stepped back from the water, giving a depth of perspective not seen anywhere else on this side of the Lough. On a bright, sunny day the sweep up to the

Greencastle

mountains is a busy network of distinctive Mourne walls and fields with farms. The land looks more restful than in other areas around Mourne. We are looking into the Kingdom of Mourne. From its south-facing beach, Greencastle is an arms length from the Cooley Peninsula and enjoys the widening expanse of the Irish Sea to one side of it and the enclosure of Carlingford Lough to the other.

The name of Cranfield has travelled well beyond its sandy beaches. During World War II, American soldiers were billeted to many posts in South Down. Many big houses became shelter for the army during their time here. They were billeted in Ballyedmond Castle, Rostrevor House and Narrow Water Castle in Warrenpoint.

Being a low lying coastal location, Cranfield offered the ideal position for an aerodrome. With the Mournes in the background and the Cooley Mountains framing the approach of aircraft to the left, this relatively sheltered expanse was an ideal location for the Air Corps which required as secluded a site as possible within these Isles for the upkeep of the fighter planes. However, the work carried out to accommodate this aspect of the war effort, necessitated demolishing 37 houses belonging to locals. Apparently, one house had just been built and the young couple were just about to move in at the time. They never got to live in their house; it with the others being knocked down to make way for the aerodrome.

Building work began in 1938 and during these war years there was employment for local men. A common sight coming into villages and towns was the arrival of the lorry to pick up men who would carry out duties to assist the soldiers in the execution of their duties at Cranfield. Thus although not directly caught up in the action, local people contributed in some way to World War II. The specific work of this aerodrome from its remote and relatively safe position was maintaining and servicing the aircraft used during the war.

On their evenings off, the soldiers, in search of entertainment travelled into the surrounding towns where music and dancing in local halls provided the opportunity to meet 'Ulster' people. The soldiers were now able to test the validity of some of the details in their Code of Conduct. They had been told to be mindful of the effect a uniform might have on a young woman and that "the male social centre in Ulster is the tavern or public house … Up in the hills you may be offered an illicit concoction known as "potheen". This is moonshine whiskey made out of potato mash. Watch it. It's dynamite…" From their Code they would have known "Wherever you go in Northern Ireland you are apt to meet a herd of sheep or cows. Remember the animals have the right of way". This was necessary information for living around South Down!

Building work at Cranfield had been completed before the official ceremony took place on 11th September 1942. It was a warm, late summer morning, when at 9.00am the soldiers paraded and stood to attention. To locals looking on from behind the walls and ditches around the fields, it seemed that there hundreds of them – all filed out and waiting. And they waited. Mid-morning came and went; midday passed by and still they waited. It got warmer, but still they stood to attention. Then, at 3.00pm the official opening ceremony took place. They had been waiting for America's First Lady, Eleanor Roosevelt, who performed the official duty at Cranfield and within 20 minutes was away.

Nowadays, people stay longer. For visitors, there is not enough time. The long beaches, the open sea, the Lough and the mountains to either side lie in wait.

Along the South Shore

Leaving Newry by its South Armagh side and heading towards Carlingford is an opportunity for you to reflect upon the fact that Co. Armagh does indeed have a coastline. As the Clanrye River leaves the city to make its way towards the Lough, it is accompanied by its historical travelling partner – The Newry Canal. The waterways run side by side separated only by a bank which rises between them. Anglers, twitchers and locals know the nesting areas on that bank. It is a hive of activity around the year, marking in the seasons, rhythms and cycles in nature. Remote from the main road through to Omeath and Carlingford, this bank provides a peaceful sanctuary – undisturbed and with only a few re-minders still visible of fixtures used to tie the craft that at one time left life a little more exposed for wildlife.

During the harsher days of deep winter, this stretch of the Canal freezes over. The open air ballet at the Albert Basin in front of The Quays stretches along the canal. Swans – always elegant – chip away at the encroaching ice with graceless determination. Their efforts on the ice surface are equally cumbersome, with webbed feet sprawling uncontrollably and going from beneath them.

But in spring, summer and autumn the Canal offers these resident birds their stage and all along its length, white plumes folded across backs, heads held high on endless necks, they faithfully glide in twos with family in line behind.

All along this route, the senses are fed by the trees, grasses, flora, bird and insect life, waterways, mountains, widening here and enclosing there. Each corner turned as you approach Omeath, offers a variation on the theme of this neck of the land – mountains and Lough, high and low.

The north facing side of the Lough is a much quieter place than its south facing coast. This is the Cooley Peninsula and although its land attachment is to the Dundalk area, its people more often look to Newry as the natural destination for shopping and cultural activities; and family ties to the North are traditionally very strong. Also, the communities on either side of the Lough see each other daily across a two mile stretch of water between Rostrevor and Carlingford and the short swim of half a mile between Omeath and Warrenpoint.

But being a peninsula it was neglected down the years after expansion in medieval times. This expansion opened up the whole area to invaders who usually came in by sea and advanced into the Carlingford Lough hinterland from its shores. As times and fortunes changed, the Cooley peninsula became a victim of the concentration on development between the main centres of Belfast and Dublin. Political events, too, dictated the pace of life for this area. Many, however, see this 'fossilisation' as a positive feature because a way of life long gone in other parts of Ireland still resonates here. Also, the streets of medieval Carlingford remain as they were designed in the Middle Ages and locals have successfully

revived an active community life around them. The strong attraction of the north-facing coast of Carlingford Lough is its obvious connection to the past.

Omeath

Omeath is the small village which is at the other end of the boat trip from Warrenpoint or the first village when travelling by road from Newry.

The early history of Omeath is tied to the Viking invasion. We have seen how the Vikings may have come to Carlingford Lough and how, at times, they continued to live around the shores for some time in peace with their Irish neighbours but it would appear that they caused great trouble for the people of Ui Meith. Having established a permanent naval base at Omeath around 851, Horm – the Viking Leader – ruled from this seat but it would be over 70 years later in 928 before Muirchertach Mac Neill known as "Hector of the West" would drive them into retreat. Some believe, moreover, that Omeath was the birthplace of one of the best known women in the medieval legends.

Iseult was the daughter of Horm who, in versions of the stories as told in medieval times, was referred to as King of Ireland who ruled over his kingdom from his settlement in Omeath. Iseult's fate became intertwined with that of Tristram, the nephew of King Mark of Cornwall. She was the bride of King Mark but unwittingly she and Tristram

View from Moygannon

drank from a love potion which doomed their love and lives. In Matthew Arnold's *Tristam and Iseult*, we learn something of the tragic love story and how Tristam - who name means 'sadness' - lay on his death bed, confused and forlorn, begging to see Iseult.

"Iseult of Brittany?--but where
Is that other Iseult fair,
That proud, first Iseult, Cornwall's queen?
She, whom Tristram's ship of yore
From Ireland to Cornwall bore,
To Tyntagel, to the side
Of King Marc, to be his bride?
She who, as they voyaged, quaff'd
With Tristram that spiced magic draught,
Which since then for ever rolls
Through their blood, and binds their souls,
Working love, but working teen?--
There were two Iseults who did sway
Each her hour of Tristram's day;
But one possess'd his waning time,
The other his resplendent prime.
Behold her here, the patient flower,
Who possess'd his darker hour!
Iseult of the Snow-White Hand
Watches pale by Tristram's bed.
She is here who had his gloom,
Where art thou who hadst his bloom?

One such kiss as those of yore
Might thy dying knight restore!
Does the love-draught work no more?
Art thou cold, or false, or dead,
Iseult of Ireland?"

The story which has provided the plot for many classical productions of the tragic love story has as it's leading lady a native of Omeath. Wagner has brought this legendary story to many with his opera 'Tristan and Isolde' and The Chieftans have immortalised the Irish link to the tragic love story. Locally, however, there seems not to have been any awareness of the connection.

Omeath was the last native Irish speaking district in North Leinster with its own Irish College in the earlier part of the 20th Century where the Park Hotel now stands. One of the reasons the Irish language remained alive in this part of the country was because the people who lived in the hills did not travel far into the anglicised parts where the speaking of Gaelige was banned. The rich oral tradition helped to preserve the folklore and poetry for which South Armagh in particular has become noted. But the speaking of Gaelige continued well into the 20th Century and began to fade only when poverty necessitated the migration to England in search of work. In his entry for the '*County Louth Archaeological Journal*', F.H.A. Aalen observes that in 1962 there 'is only one old person [who] speaks the language'. Speaking Gaelige

Omeath Shoreline

had become associated with the poor who tended to be hill dwellers and the growth in tourism coupled with the clerical opposition to the speaking of Gaelige contributed further to its decline.

But Omeath contributed to the tradition of poetry in the wider district during the 17th and 18th centuries. The South Ulster School of Poets, as they were known, came from Louth, Armagh, Meath and Monaghan. There were six 'major' poets – Turlough O'Carolan, Peadar O'Doirnin, Sean O'Neachtain, Art MacCooey, Patrick MacAlinden and most respected of all – Seumas MacCuarta from Omeath. There were many other 'minor' poets and singers who kept the culture alive and recorded by word of mouth the details of songs and poetry few of which now remain. During the time of the Irish Language over two hundred and fifty songs were documented, thirty-four of which were published in *Ceolta Omeith*. The Irish College, which opened on August 22nd 1912, was built on the site from where it is said that the early Irish leader Muirchertach of the Leathern Cloaks drove one of the Vikings clans into the sea.

As this is a peninsula with a close relationship to the North, events in the North impacted for better or worse. The economy of the village was principally seasonal. However World War II brought much activity to the village. The Red Star was a ferry company operated by the O'Neills in Warrenpoint. Daily crossings carried visitors on the ten minute crossing

and while the busiest time for Omeath was during World War II it was not with military activity; whatever about the legal status of their actions, many older people reminisce about the ingenuity in smuggling! Butter, sausages, bacon, blades, alcohol – in fact, all the goods that were rationed during the war years found their way into Northern Ireland via Omeath. One woman from Belfast remembers with fondness the feeling of being wrapped around the body with sausages. The merchants were keen to assist their customers in whatever way they could.

CARLINGFORD

The road leaving Omeath for Carlingford rises to a height which gives a twofold sensation of distance: an early full view to the lowlands at the foot of the Mournes running down and out to the mouth of the Lough contrasts with the closeness of soft hills of the low Mournes behind Rostrevor and Killowen.

Coming to the final rise on the road, just before the steep descent into the medieval town of Carlingford, on the left-hand side tucked in beneath is Carlingford Marina. The Marina is a magnet for the boating and sailing community around the Lough. It is a social centre for all of Carlingford Lough and on the days when competitions are taking place, either here or the short distance away at the Southern Education and Library Board's Outdoor Pursuits Centre across at Killowen, the Lough is a confetti of sails.

Carlingford Harbour

An interesting vessel is docked at Carlingford Marina – a Concrete Boat. The *Crete Gath* was built in 1920 and is one of the many concrete boats built in those days to replace lost tonnage from World War I. Originally built as a steam tug to take paper to the Isle of Man, it was converted after a time to store grain. It ended up on the River Boyne in Drogheda before being brought to Carlingford Lough in 1980 where it was used as a boom to protect the marina during its construction.

Concrete ships were built all around the world in those days. Indeed, across the lough at Warrenpoint, before ship building ceased there in the late '40s, three concrete boats were built and used for hauling munitions during World War II.

The road into Carlingford passes under a bridge which was built in 1874 and therefore a feature of the developments in the region to improve the infrastructure. Originally designed as the right of way into the town for the new line of the Dundalk – Newry – Greenore Railway, it became the main road after the railway closure in 1951. A visitor could well believe this grand entrance to be part of the medieval town wall, such is its stature. But that is not the case.

Carlingford was a vibrant town in the Middle Ages as it was the ship port for traders during the 14th, 15th and 16th centuries. A map drawing of the town in 1642 – and referred to in manuscript plans in the British Library as 'O'Hanlon's Cuntrie' – shows Carlingford with a wall surrounding a compact stand of reasonably sized buildings overlooking Carlingford Lough. The illustration confirms what we now know from historical research that this was a well developed, orderly and managed working centre. This early industry fell away with the development of the trading centre at Newry but a combination of factors – being on a peninsula, demise of infrastructure and political and social instability in the surrounding district, left Ireland with what many antiquarians consider to be the richest of medieval centres.

Like all castles, it took some time to complete the building. It was wife-to-be of Hugh de Lacy who choose this site – a promontory with limited space, rising above the waters of the Lough and giving views to the south, north and east. In 1195 the building began and by 1210 he had completed the west portion. King John came to visit in July and August of that year and so it became forever King John's Castle. It took another 51 years to complete the east portion and in 1261 there stood the Castle which was to mark Carlingford out as a medieval centre of some significance for centuries to come.

The impressive 45 feet high dividing wall, has a 13 feet base batter tapering to 9 feet at the top. Still visible through protective visitor gates, is the courtyard where the soldiers worked. Beyond the courtyard lay the banqueting hall which led down to the domestic part of the castle. Into the right

King John's Castle

were the bed chambers. Although visitors now cannot see them, there exist some remains of the stairways within the Castle's original walls.

It was three centuries before King John's Castle was revamped. In the early 15th Century some of the rooms were divided and fireplaces were installed. But these more comfortable conditions were enjoyed for a short time only. Under Cromwell's orders, Captain Venables sacked a lot of the castles, taking armaments from them. Consequently, very little has been left for the historians and archaeologists. By 1689, the town had become demilitarised.

Just beyond the bridge to the right, a medieval streetscape remains as it has been for centuries. Narrow streets, burgages lanes and squares bring the walker around the walled town. Edward II in 1326 granted permission to build a town wall. Such walls were built not only as defences but also as boundaries between Gaels and Normans. Carlingford had 12 burgages or sovereigns who were freemen of the town and they made the laws. A plot of land was hired out and known as a burgages plot. The lanes between these plots remain. To the back of the uppermost street, a small portion of the original town wall remains visible and is part of a contemporary back garden. Originally this piece of the wall stood at 20 metres long, 3 metres high and 1.5 metres thick. Gun loops are still visible on the remaining portion which dates it to the early part of the 15th Century.

The narrow winding streets run down to the square. Under Royal Charter in Medieval times, Carlingford was granted permission to hold an annual fair between 25th and 28th August. At the beginning of its recent renaissance, this date was honoured once more and in August 1982 the first Carlingford Oyster Festival was held. For 12 years it attracted thousands of visitors to this almost forgotten slice of Medieval Ireland on the Cooley Peninsula.

One of the most photographed petrol pumps in the world stands on the corner of a beautiful medieval street – Tholsel Street – at PJ O'Hare's Pub. Traffic is no longer served but this quaint piece of street furniture is a fond reminder of mid 20th Century economic development. It is now a feature in countless holiday images which have travelled home to every corner of the earth. In a very strategic position, next to the family pub built in 1864, it ushers the visitor onto the street where Medieval administration business took place.

A short distance and to the right hand side stands the Mint. In 1467 Carlingford was granted the right under

The Tholsel

View of the Lough from Greenore

charter to mint its own coinage. It is unclear whether coins were actually minted here as none had ever been found. There is the possibility that documents were formulated here or indeed that it was a clearing house for money or coins. The building certainly had significance as the well preserved window decorations testify. The detail on the corners illustrate images influenced by the Celtic Renaissance Art – very clearly visible is interlace on the upper left-hand and a bust of a man on the upper right-hand sides of one of the windows. Other details reflect trading activity of the time. It is believed that a wealthy merchant family may have lived in this building.

Appropriately, the Mint was built in local limestone – particular to the Cooley Peninsula – and it stands up to its original height. The road below, however, was about two metres deeper than the current thoroughfare. In such an enclosed, narrow street it would have been an impressive looking establishment.

Towards the end of the street, the eponymous Tholsel stands two storeys high. There is little doubt that there was a third level in the original building. The room above the gateway was the venue for the burgages meetings and in the tight, cramped conditions

the town's laws were formulated. But not so confined as the gaol which is at the left-hand foot of the Tholsel. Peering through the locked gate, the tiny, dark cell devoid of natural light stills gives a strong impression of the fate meted out to the criminal who would spend a night there before execution by hanging next day!

Walking through the archway, the visitor leaves behind medieval Carlingford and moves out into Gaelige Ireland. Standing directly opposite is the distinctive, white Ghann House. An L shaped Georgian building, it takes its name from the gaelige meaning for 'poor land by the sea'. The house was built by William Stannus and was later acquired by the Rutherfords, agents for the absentee landlord Lord Anglesey. Many of the original features of the house remain intact, for example the vaulted basement with its semi circular windows at ground level, several Georgian fireplaces and rococo plaster work in the drawing room ceiling. The Carroll Family now own it and run their cookery school and guest house business.

Carlingford Lough may well have come in shore closer to Ghann house than it does presently. The main road running from Newry to Greenore passes along the route created for the 19th Century railway. But the Tower House on the right just inside the main bridge at King John's Castle, has features which confirm this. Paddy Small lives in this house and the opening to the basement entrance which is visible from the

Docks at Greenore

road, are heavy, arched, wooden doors which were designed to open down to the waters of Carlingford Lough. It is obvious from the well preserved interior arched roof that this was where the boat was kept.

The main road travels towards Greenore – now as always a busy port. Greenore is a busy, commercial shipping port at the mouth of Carlingford Lough on the southern side. Bypassed in favour of the more strategic setting of Carlingford by the early settlers, Greenore lay quiet until 1867 when it first opened as a passenger and freight link to Britain.

This put the village on the map as yet another doorway on Carlingford Lough. It made sense, therefore, to roll out the train line to this destination in 1873, linking Newry and Dundalk to the deep sea port. Although the train line no longer exists, the shadow of those times is well defined by its streets and hotel building, pristine and functional.

Newry

Iur Cinn – Yew Tree at the Head of the Strand – is Newry. Sitting in a valley with the Mourne Mountains to the east, Carlingford Mountains to the south, Slieve Gullion and Camlough Mountain to the west, the city of Newry has been growing for almost ten centuries. In the days when invaders came in by sea, the strand made it a challenging place to put down significant roots for settlement and with Carlingford so well positioned on the Lough that was the obvious landing point for early visitors. This valley with its marshy terrain, however, was to grow to become the main centre in the region. In its embryonic stage it offered little more than access to water to the first interested party and it was a meeting place for traders and farmers. As it happened, water was to become a key ingredient in the building up of the fortunes of Newry.

The name, *Iur Cinn Tragh*, is a reference to St. Patrick who is said to have visited Newry in the 5th Century and planted a yew tree to mark his presence. St. Patrick visited many places in Ireland but in Newry he is remembered by the coat of arms which depicts him seated with mitre and a yew tree to either side of him.

The Monks

As well as the more positive aspects of their legacy, the Vikings left a lot of turmoil and confusion in their wake. However, Newry itself was spared the direct influence of these invaders. During the 11th Century, the Gateway to Ulster was well placed for further development and growth. With regular markets and fairs in the valley, Newry became the meeting point for farmers and dwellers who came to trade at a central location. With so many traffic routes on land and sea leading to this marshland at the head of Carlingford Lough, it was only a matter of time before a settled community was established.

Preparation for the approaching opportunities was heralded by the arrival of Benedictine Monks who arrived in Ireland in 1135. The Benedictine's need to settle in a place remote from people but suitable in its surroundings to support the life of a community of monks, meant that Newry was ideal. A few of the monks settled here. Their influence was so great that the blessing of St. Benedict was invoked in the Charter that established an Abbey for a branch of the Benedictine order, the Cistercians, at Newry. *Mael Maedoc*, later known as St. Malachy, had a significant role in bringing the Cistercian Monks to Ireland coming to Nerwy in 1144.

Their influence was immediately felt. They reviewed the harsh ways of earlier customs and the old order began to fall away in favour of a more acceptable approach to managing life. In 1157, Murtagh MacLoughlin granted a Charter to the abbey. The Charter granted them ownership of all of Newry. An 1876 translation of the original text is contained in 'Newrensis':

Charta Abbatiae de Newry

Maurice MacLoughlin, King of all Ireland, to all its Kings, Princes, Nobles, Leaders, Clergy, Laity and to all and each present and to come, greeting:

Know ye that I, by the unanimous will and common consent …

… have granted and confirmed in honour of the Blessed Virgin Mary, Saint Patrick and Saint Benedict, the father and founder of the Cistercian Order to the Monks serving God in Nyvorcintracta as a perpetual and pure donation, the land of O'Cormaic whereon was founded a monastery…

The charter references the townlands of Sheeptown, Carnmeen, Crobane and Croreagh, Corcreehy and Greenan as part of the gift. Murtagh MacLoughlin invited anyone who had land to consider donating it for 'the health of their souls'.

This development formalised their presence and marked the recognition of a viable community with customs and traditions which were to continue to grow in shaping the identity of the early Newry and Carlingford Lough community.

A monastic establishment which contained wood and thatch housed the Cistercian Monks. The Europeans had approached the design and layout of their buildings with function in mind. (Interestingly, in modern times and further round the coast at Rostrevor, a Benedictine Monastery has been built in 2003-2004. In designing that monastery, the architect lived with the community for three or four days to ascertain their needs in order to provide them with appropriate accommodation for 21st Century living. What he discovered to his bemusement was that the early design was the best one suited to communal living.) As now, the first monastery in the area was laid out with Church, kitchen and refectory arranged around the cloister on the ground floor. The monks' accommodation was located on the upper floor. Work needed to maintain a rhythm of life for them and those living in Newry was carried out under the shadow of the building which was the site of one of the two yew trees apparently planted by St. Patrick in previous times. It is thought that this first dwelling was erected on Castle Street where it meets Abbey Yard. And the first Abbot of Newry was Finn, son of Gorman, who later went on to be Bishop of Kildare. But in 1162 disaster struck when the building was burned destroying furniture, books and one of St. Patrick's yew trees. But the Cistercian presence continued and became a central feature in the life of the town.

Over the next few centuries, Newry continued to occupy a place of strategic interest to the rulers and armies who came to Ireland. In 1237, under Hugh de Lacy, Newry was burned to the ground but the fortunes of the area were determined by the policies and actions of those who came after him. Land was given to the representatives of the Crown in order to shift the culture and secure loyalty.

The next significant point in Newry's history was the arrival of Nicholas Bagenal. Historians agree that this was the beginning of a productive period in the life of the Gateway to Ulster.

Bagenal

Bagenal is the name of the man, who, in the Middle Ages, began the process of unifying the land and the people immediately around the Carlingford Lough area. This colourful man was appointed by the Crown to oversee the rooting into this area by the then invaders, and was posted to Newry. He was also given the gift of the land around Omeath and Carlingford to govern and subsequently another gift of land out to Greencastle was passed over to him. So, we can trace more recent community links to that time and reveal something of the connectedness which begins to unfold from then around the economic and cultural developments of South Down, South Armagh and North County Louth. Whatever about the land boundaries and borders, the water washing the shores is the element that binds us together.

It is not uncommon to hear local people speak disparagingly of Nicholas Bagenal. It was said that he had a criminal record for having committed many murders. The exact truth and circumstances of this lie covered in mystery because historians have found very little reference to the crimes. What appears to have happened is that he was involved in a 'brawl' with 'light people' and a murder was committed. What ever the truth, he came to Ireland as a fugitive and it was this detail in his CV which later deprived Newry of its first real opportunity to grow into a significant, prominent centre within the British Isles.

Nicholas Bagenal came to Ireland in 1539 where he entered the employment of the O'Neills as a mercenary soldier. This has led some historians to the belief that he operated as a double agent for the Crown. With O'Neill playing a key role in having Bagenal pardoned of his crimes, the suspicion maybe valid. The submission contains these words:

'... the said Nicholas hither fled and has
since done very honest service'.

Thus indicating the high esteem in which he was held – for whatever reason – by the O'Neills. The application to the Privy Council was successful and pardon was granted on 2nd March 1543.

'Nicholas Bagenal, or Bagnolde, or Bagenholde, late
of Wolston, Warwickshire, alias of Warwicke, alias
of Stafford, alias of Langforde Derbyshire, Yeoman.
General pardon of all murders by him committed.'

This marked a major turning in events in the life of Nicholas Bagenal and of Newry.

This son of the Mayor of Newcastle-under-Lyme rose through the ranks of the military and ruling class in Ireland to arrive at the post of Marshal of the King's Army. He progressed quickly to the Privy Council of Ireland and was considered suitable material for heading up the developments around Carlingford Lough. The English Privy Council made him a lease of 'The Newrye' for a 21 year period. Within two years, the potential of this area was apparent to the rulers and Bagenal's 21 year lease was converted to a more permanent arrangement. Newry has been recognised as having strategic importance and the English Crown worked very hard to keep it under its wing.

The earlier support from the O'Neills seems to have evaporated by this stage when we consider that after his arrival in Newry he was routinely attacked by them. Many letters dating from that time to his superiors record just how difficult the O'Neills were making life for him in Newry. It was very difficult for Bagenal for some years as his good fortunes wavered and he became exasperated by their attempts to remove him. This situation was further compounded by his having fallen out of favour with the Tudors. During Queen Mary's reign, he was stripped of his title and it was some time before Queen Elizabeth restored it in 1565. Bagenal's troubles were such – particularly at the hands of Shane O'Neill – that he vowed to sell up and move out. This move was not part of the Crown's plan for Newry and Carlingford Lough. Here was an area of strategic importance and Bagenal was convinced to remain.

His troubles abated on the death of Shane O'Neill in 1567 and in the peaceful times which followed, Bagenal was able to concentrate on the job of establishing Newry as a town although his favourite residence was at Greencastle. He found relative peace there from his troubles and it was there he died in 1590. His remains were buried at St. Patrick's Church, Newry.

But it would seem that fate had predestined the links between the O'Neills and the Bagenals because a year after his death, Nicholas' daughter Mabel was married to Hugh O'Neill of Tyrone. Now, this was a marriage which Henry, Nicholas' son and now Marshal of the Army in Ireland, considered unsuitable. His sister Mabel was only sixteen years old and Hugh O'Neill was in his mid forties, but the fact that she had fallen in love with one of the clan which had made so much trouble for his father was a greater offence. Henry Bagenal had great difficulty in accepting any attempt of Hugh O'Neill's to become part of the family.

Henry was right to be suspicious of O'Neill who treated Mabel appallingly from early on in the marriage. Before long, Mabel learned that he had at least two mistresses at Dungannon. Her life turned sour and she died of heart disease at the early age of 21. It is said that she died a Catholic and estranged from her family.

Of the many mysteries surrounding the enigmatic Bagenal one has recently been solved. When Bagenal came to Newry first, he would have had to settle in or near to the place where a community already existed but despite much legend and lore modern historians had been unable to pinpoint the location of his residence.

As the centuries passed, the old part of Newry – where any such residence would most likely have been located – came to encompass Church Street, High Street, North Street and Castle Street. Once this was a busy complex of housing, markets and shops. A network of alleyways linked this area to the back of the dam (Water Street) and Hill Street. A lot of this old part was ripped out during the '60s to create a main through road for traffic between Belfast and Dublin. It was mainly the businesses on North Street which vanished and with them all the artefacts of the retail trade in Newry from the 18th and 19th centuries. This demolition is still referred to with regret by many locals. One quaint artefact has survived and it was replaced in recent years to it's original position: the Golden Teapot that is on the corner wall of what was formerly Kelly and Calverts', family grocers, in Margaret Square.

Castle Street, however, was spared during the demolition. On it stood McCann's Bakery which, from small beginnings in 1837, grew to be a major employer and a household name. It seemed that there were only two types of bread in Newry and the surrounding area: home-made and McCann's.

However after 160 years of baking in Newry, the family run business closed in 1997. But what became revealed

when the sale of the premises was being completed, threw new light on Newry's history and excited archaeologists, historians and locals. Down the years, walls had been erected inside the bakery to create much needed space for ovens. Unwittingly – but perhaps fortuitously – the original building was being concealed and what was uncovered confirmed the hunch some historians had about a castle built in the vicinity by Bagenal. Indeed, employees of the Bakery had at times uncovered some artefacts in the grounds and local knowledge was confident about Bagenal's Castle having been there. The warm ovens kept some original walls with plaster intact and architectural features of the 16th Century are clearly visible.

This find has been acknowledged as one of the most significant in Ireland for a long time. In her small information book, Museum Curator Noreen Cunningham says:

"Uniquely it has the oldest known set of original floor plans and perspective drawings that survive for a standing building in Ireland … They are attributed to the English engineer and surveyor Robert Lythe and are believed to date to around 1568. The plans survived as they were sent to London, and the originals are located in the Public Records Office at Kew".

The castle links Newry with the Cistercian Monks. It had been thought that Bagenal had simply occupied the existing Abbey, but this find has revealed a basement filled in with masonry which will doubtless clarify the story. In Newry, it is said that Bagenal demolished the Abbot's house and built a stronger dwelling instead. Scientific analysis of the rubble beneath the 16th Century floor may confirm the folklore. What is visible, however, are the window outlines, a large fireplace – perhaps in a banqueting room, the internal wall faces, a set of steps leading to the basement, internal wall carvings and a cross engraved on granite which some believe may have come from the original Abbot's House.

This Newry's oldest surviving building is being converted to a Museum for the whole district.

The Market

As with most other towns and villages up and down the country, the market features prominently in the weekly calendar. Throughout the years, all roads lead to Newry with the promise of intense trading and endless socialising. Townspeople looked forward to the influx of near neighbours and the links to each other were consolidated across the spit and handshake of many a deal. The long tradition of open air trading at the head of the strand, dates Newry's market to be the oldest in Europe standing on its original site.

The Market is at the foot of Hill Street on the right hand side next to Philips' – a long standing family fish, fruit and vegetable business. These days, Newry Market is open on Thursdays and Saturdays and adds to the rich commercial life of a rapidly changing new city. So embedded is the market in the collective mind of the area that Thursday has become the traditional day for 'going to Newry'. The variety market attracts a network of stall holders, some of whom regard improvised entertainment as part of customer service. One of the more memorable in this genre was a man named Hector. Much to my amazement as a child, he ran

his business from a large lorry. With back doors flung open to the prospective purchasers and showing off what appeared to be endless supplies of quality household goods, Hector invited bids on selected items held up for all to see and with determined application, talked his way into the purse of converted shoppers. More disciplined visitors studied his style and marvelled at the bravery of anyone who dared to express a thought or challenge the price. Here was the chance to listen to sharpened wit and two-way public dialogue. The market was always alive, noisy and busy.

Today we have one location for the Market. However, 130 years ago, one day might not have given enough time to tour the eight regular markets in the town. Bye-laws for the 'Regulation of the Markets and Fairs' dated 11th August 1874 lists locations and permitted goods for sale at the various Markets. Currently known as Patrick's Street, Needham

Street's Market sold 'Wheat, Barley, Bere, Oats, Rye, Beans, Peas, Vetches, Flaxseed, Oatmeal, Wheatmeal, Barleymeal, Beanmeal, Peasmeal, Ryemeal, Seeds, Groats, Oat-chaff, Grass-seed, Pork, Tow and Hemp etc.'

A second market at Needham Street was the live pig and sheep Market. Details stipulate: 'For the sale of live pigs on foot, creel or cart pigs, sheep, slink and veal calves'. Butter Crane Quay Market was the third listed – this land mark has been revived again in the late 20th Century as a shopping centre. As the name indicates, butter was the produce 'in firkins, butts, crocks, boxes and barrels.'

Mary Street had two markets and it is likely that this was the location of Newry's first Market place. At the South Market on Mary Street, vegetables – including 'Mangle Wurzel' – and all classes of edible flesh went on sale. Meanwhile, at the North Market, hay, straw, turf, bogwood, flax-bands, vetches, grass, clover and green feeding for cattle could be bought. This was also the place to find the cooper, woodturner and carpenter at work.

Hide Terrace Market provided space for the sale of old and new furniture and 'Wearing Apparel, Marine Stores.' The Hiring Market was held in Mary Street; and Market Street Market, which opened up to High Street, down to Mill Street and into Castle Street, was where 'Print and

Lump Butter, Cheese and Eggs' were sold along side a Retail Market for fruit and vegetables.

The first Monday of each month was instituted as the Fair Day. This was when 'horses, black cattle, calves, sheep, lambs, goats, mule or ass, hog or pig and other live stock' were sold in the Markets at Needham Street.

From the details, it is clear that the hinterland around Newry contributed substantially to the commercial life of the town. A web of connections grew out of this style of doing business. Urban and rural lives became fused through the exchange of news, views and marriage vows. There was a lot of traffic milling around the town and a journey to Newry often required musical instruments – just in case you had to entertain yourself while the horse was being shod at the blacksmith's. A spontaneous ceili arose from hanging around waiting. Music underscored the proceedings of Market Day in Newry.

Worship in Newry

During the time of Nicholas Bagenal, substantial effort was put into developing a trading town. Features of prosperity began to appear – the town was walled in defence against enemies, English settlers were introduced, commercial activity was encouraged and, most significantly in those times, perhaps, Ireland's first purpose built Protestant Church was built in 1578.

St. Patrick's Church is in the old part of Newry. The corner of Stream Street and Church Street overlooks Newry and St. Patrick's stands on the rise above the Church graveyard. As with all the plans he had proposed for Newry, Bagenal was frustrated in his attempts to get funding from Elizabeth I for the Church. Undeterred in his zeal to put Newry on the map, he put his own resources into the project. He spared no expense in providing a place of worship which was furnished to the highest standard. The carved stone work of the Church building added to the grandeur and the Bagenal coat of arms was installed.

St. Patrick's Church was destroyed during the fire of 1689. For some time, it lay derelict and was partially rebuilt in 1720 and in 1866 it was restored.

A visit to the graveyard provides a roll call of Newry family names from early times and, of course, Bagenal's remains were laid to rest there.

The second ecclesiastical building to be established was in High Street. This was the Meeting House of the Presbyterians in Newry, built in 1722.

Presbyterians first came to Newry with the Scottish Army of General Monroe in 1650 during times of trouble. Unfortunately, their experience in Ireland over the following decade was an unhappy and unsettled one. Both Presbyterians and Catholics became victims of oppression by the ruler and an attempt to rid Counties Antrim and Down of senior Presbyterians led to seven ministers being imprisoned in Carlingford before returning them to Scotland.

In Newry, the congregation continued to meet at a place on the Belfast Road, known as Meeting House Rocks. While outside the town itself, they enjoyed some security. As it happened, it was fortuitously located because the fire which burned Newry to the ground did not spread to the outskirts. The Presbyterian Meeting House was untouched.

This troublesome background to their establishment in Newry is indicative of a tenacity which would later benefit the growth and prosperity of the town. After the Boyne victory, Newry was rebuilt and the Presbyterian Congregation grew in number and material comfort. As in other parts of the country, they contributed to the emerging merchant culture which was a boon to the creative entrepreneur. Before very long, their increasing numbers could no longer be accommodated at The Meeting House Rocks. Business acumen and partnership produced the revenue and purpose necessary to build a new Meeting House. And with the help of Lord Kilmorey who leased them land in High Street, Newry's second ecclesiastical building was established in 1722.

This was a large building with over an acre of land for a

graveyard. On a map from those times, the Meeting House is identified by a large cruciform which confirms the belief that the congregation was large in number. Over the following years, the Presbyterian Congregation remained active in worship and among the invited preachers was founder of the Methodists, Rev. John Wesley. In 1756 he recorded his positive impressions of Newry comparing it favourably to Liverpool, which at that time was Britain's largest port.

The most notable name from the Presbyterian Community and a major figure in Ireland politics was the Patriot - John Mitchel.

The remains of the Meeting House with family graves – including the families Mitchel, Scott, Hill, Frazer and Warnock – are in the grounds of the Poor Clare Convent in High Street, a street which in the first stage of its growth was one of the busiest in the town.

Until the early 1980s, one Catholic graveyard served it's congregation in Newry. It is attached to what is known as 'The Old Chapel'. This is St. Mary's Chapel and contrary to what is implied, it was in fact a 'new' chapel to replace the original St. Mary's.

Lord Kilmorey granted the lease of land to Catholics who, along side their Presbyterian colleagues, were experiencing a similar turn around in fortunes. They had embraced the opportunities presented by commercial confidence and many of the Catholic merchants, having now become wealthy, were in position to provide Newry with its third ecclesiastical building in the 1740s.

Originally, St. Mary's was erected in Boat Street. The proximity of the chapel to where the river and the canal met guaranteed convenience of worship for those engaged in trading. The town continued to grow, was busier by the year and the population increase meant overcrowding in Boat Street's St. Mary's. Chapel Street became the preferred location for the replacement Catholic Church and the new chapel was built in the 1790s.

In this graveyard, too, you will find many Newry family names from generations past. The traditional blue slate headstones from the 1800s still hold the engraved details of names, birth and death dates.

This new chapel became the 'Old Chapel' when the Catholic Cathedral of St. Patrick and St. Colman was completed in 1829. The first Cathedral in Ireland to be opened after Catholic emancipation, it's Gothic features reflect strong European influence. Indeed, in the late 20th Century, when the mosaic floor of the Cathedral was in need of repair, the absence of local expertise required skilled mosaic workers to travel from Italy to carry out the job.

St. Patrick's Church

Newry Canal

It would be very difficult to imagine Newry without the Canal. And yet this unique waterway – which runs along side the Clanrye River through the city – was excavated as recently as the 18th Century to accommodate the transport of coal from Tyrone to Dublin. The Newry Canal is an integral part of the life and history of the city because it helped to generate substantial economic growth making it the fourth largest port in Ireland and the largest in Ulster. This artery was Newry's lifeline.

The first suggestion for a 'navigable trench' came from Colonel George Monck, an officer in Cromwell's army, in the 1640s. It was accepted that there would be great potential in developing the idea into a workable plan. But nothing happened. In 1703 Francis Nevil, Collector of HM Revenues in Ireland, presented a survey to Parliament of the land between Lough Neagh and Newry and included a design of a drawing of a canal. Once again, this good idea was shelved. But we hear about it again in 1715 when an act of Parliament was passed to encourage inland navigation with the purpose of benefiting the River Liffey. So, 1729 saw the establishment of Commissioners of Inland Navigation for Ireland and by early 1731 work on the digging out of the 18 mile long channel had begun under the supervision of HM Engineer and Surveyor General Sir Edward Lovett Pearce.

The task in hand was a formidable one: 18 miles in length, 40 feet wide, 6 feet deep, climbing to a height of 78 feet above sea level, retaining an even depth of water along its entire length which would have 14 locks – and all work carried out in pre-industrial revolution times, therefore using shovels, picks and sweat from long hours on a seasonal rota for 7$^\text{d}$ per day. The project benefited greatly from the appointment of French Huguenot Richard Castle who had arrived in Ireland with extensive knowledge from engineering and canal construction in Germany. Castle replaced Pearce who had died in 1733. And a further feature of note was the fact that this was the FIRST canal of its type in the British Isles. It was the template which would inform the future web of canals around Ireland and Britain. Little wonder, then, that the Newry Canal appears in the Guinness Book of Records.

The Town Hall

Toward the end of the 19th Century, Newry was well established as the main town between Belfast and Dublin and as such, there was a need to provide the locality with a building which would signify and capture the important business of managing its civic affairs and provide a much needed venue. 1893 with the building work complete, the new Town Hall bridged the gap opened up by the conundrum: A town standing in two counties – where to place it? Apparently, there was some dispute over the location of a municipal building which was to serve everyone in Newry – the challenge was embraced creatively with the plan to

Newry Canal

build it straddling the Clanrye River. So, residents of the Co. Armagh part of Newry and those of the Co. Down part of the town could equally claim the new building as theirs. It stands, appropriately, on the Armagh-Down Bridge.

William Batt was the architect of this redbrick building and the contractor was David Mahood. It is a solid building reflecting the business it has guarded down the years. Ornate gates open into an entrance hallway with heavy half glass doors which in turn sweep up to the stairways rising to either side of the foyer and lead to the performance hall on the first floor. The stage was designed to professional specifications and amateur performers quickly grasp the technique of walking on a 'slope'! A slight gradient running to the front of the wooden stage floor is designed to create perspective. This is added value to the training of many performers who subsequently went on to work professionally in the arts.

On the ground floor, the Boardroom was formerly home to Council meetings before the building of O'Hagan House on Monaghan Row which is one of two sites of the District Council Offices. In the foyer stands a bust of Lord Charles Russell, of Killowen who rose to the rank of Lord Chief Justice of England. A portrait hangs there, too, of August (Gus) Toremans, an Austrian musician who came to Newry as a young music teacher in the 1940s and stayed. Gus Toremans was very much at home in the music theatre which was rapidly growing in Newry at that time.

Recent refurbishment in the 1990s brightened the interior and equipped the building to serve the needs of all its users. Most striking is the decor of the performance hall itself. A ceiling of midnight blue is relieved by embossed gold stars, deep blue window drapes block out daylight and on the exterior skirt of the balcony is written four lines from the first stanza of *Ode* by Arthur O'Shaughnessy:

We are the music makers,
And we are the makers of dreams …
Yet we are the movers and shakers
Of the world for ever, it seems.

A constant reminder from the 19th Century Irish poet of the true role of the arts in our affairs.

Performing Arts

Newry Town Hall provided the first stage for thousands of Feis competitors in entertaining audiences.

Having a venue in the Town Hall was the cue that was needed to prompt performance again in Newry. In the first half of the 20th Century three organisations were to open doors for many people of the region who otherwise might not have realised their creative potential.

Newry Musical Feis was set up in 1928. In those early days, music was the principle event at the annual competi-

Newry Town Hall

tion. But the popularity of the Feis and the demand for a wider spectrum of performing arts dictated growth. Irish dancing and Speech and Drama were incorporated into the programme and attracted participants from all over Ireland. This gave local talent the opportunity to stretch itself to the highest standards because teachers from Dublin, who were preparing students for the young Irish Theatre of the time, encouraged the journey to Newry. The competition was challenging and most of the awards stayed within the Newry And Carlingford Lough area – a measure of the professionalism of local teachers in these fields. Adjudicators, too, were keen to take up the offer of presiding over the competitions. Well known names included Sam McCready and Betty-Ann Norton.

Newry Feis continued to develop and embrace all the performing arts which young people were keen to have recognised through formal competition.

But, the Feis was not only about competing.

"At a Festival, Competitors do not set out to beat each other, they set out to pace each other on the road to perfection" – Sir H. Walford Davies. The reminder to all which is printed on the cover of the Feis programme of what it is really about. It provides young people with the opportunity to engage with each other through the arts and to learn great names and pieces of work from literature, music, theatre and dance. Many examples of the finest extracts from plays, poetry, scores and dances are now firmly lodged in the memory bank of thousands of former competitors. Anyone who has ever walked on to that stage will never forget the heart-stopping wait for the adjudicator's bell, the cue to begin to perform to an attentive audience of parents, teachers, friends and members of the public whose love of live theatre was satisfied for a couple of weeks annually.

Brenda Fricker, Gerard Lynch, Aislinn Sands, Seamus Crimmins and John Toal are a few of the local people who performed in their early years at Newry Feis and who went on to become highly respected both nationally and internationally in their respective creative careers.

But the Town Hall was not the only arts venue. Newry's first publicly performed play was *The Inconstant* by James Farquhar in 1769. High Street was a busy place in the 18th and 19th centuries and was the obvious venue for a theatre.

James Porter converted a building for use as the town's original theatre on ground quite close to where the Convent of Poor Clares now stands and close to an inn called 'The Pope's Head'. The theatre attracted acting companies from Belfast and Dublin, so from early days the tradition of performance was a strong feature in the life of the city. Within 14 years a purpose built theatre was built on Hill Street.

In 1783 at 71-73 Hill Street a grand ball was hosted by Thomas Betterton. He was the manager and owner of The Theatre Royal and the celebratory Ball was its first event. Thereafter, the theatre provided space for performers who continued to include Newry on their itinerary as they travelled between Dublin and Belfast. The purpose built theatre offered patrons and actors top quality facilities comparable to those in the capital. It had a reputation which sustained it for one hundred years worth of audiences. Unfortunately, the owner-manager put on a less productive performance. Troublesome bookkeeping resulted in he and his family having to leave Newry to join a travelling theatre company after incurring substantial debt for The Theatre Royal. A well known actor of that time – Julia Betterton – was born to Thomas in 1779 in Hill Street. The Betterton family stayed in theatre and with true dramatic irony returned to perform in Newry some years later to the place which they had established. Their Newry audience contributed generously to a benefit performance for actors in straitened circumstances!

The curtain came down on the Theatre Royal on Hill Street in 1832.

As the years went by, the need to build on what was being encouraged in the Feis became apparent. Also, there is more than one road to the bright lights! In 1945, the Newry Musical and Orchestral Society pulled together the collective disciplines within the arts scene and under it's first president W.V. Hogg Snr. performed *The Mikado*. This was the beginning of a long run for the NMOS of shows which could only otherwise be seen by travelling to a main city or in the cinema.

But more valuable still, was the wealth of amateur talent front of stage and backstage. The progression from formalised one-piece-performance at the Feis, blossomed into a collective of set designers, costume makers, make-up artists, producers and directors, musicians, choreographers and lighting technicians, singers, dancers and actors. In the days when Newry was a small town, every street could boast someone taking part in that year's production.

Newpoint Players was established in 1946. This drama company satisfied the need for a different type of performance – more serious, intense and initially script only. Their inaugural production communicated this message clearly. It was Shakespeare's *A Midsummer Night's Dream* in 1949. Over the years, various plays tested players and kept Newry audiences in touch with the more reflective work of theatre. But the name which has become synonymous with the Newpoint Players is Sean Hollywood – acknowledged as being the driving force which propelled many young people in the '80s and '90s into professional theatre, cinema, television and radio. Sean Hollywood demanded professionalism from the amateurs involved. The evidence of the high standard of the performing arts in the Newry area can be seen in the numbers of people who went on to work professionally in the field. Sean Kearns, Kieran Cunningham, John Lynch and Susan Lynch first became involved in theatre locally and subsequently moved into film, television and stage productions.

Newry and Mourne's Arts Centre – appropriately renamed The Sean Hollywood Arts Centre in honour of his contribution to the arts life of the area – adjacent to the City Hall, has exhibition space for art and photography clubs of the Newry, Mourne and Carlingford Lough area. The auditorium space holds 120 -170, offering a smaller venue than the performance space in the City Hall. Rehearsal rooms, a workshop and studios indicate a vibrant cultural life in an area where people have long enjoyed the arts.

When we step back to look at the broader picture of this whole region, the pulse of creativity has always been evident. From Carlingford around the coastline to Greencastle, singers like La Scala performer Marjorie Wright, Voice of Ireland Ros O'Dhubhain, Eurovision song entrant Clodagh Rodgers; composers and song writers eg Eilish Farrell, Tommy and Colum Sands, Michael Durkin, Fil Campbell; visual artists for example Colum McEvoy, Heather Grills, Sean Hillen; countless musicians and photographers have featured in the smaller histories of townlands and villages. They act as ambassadors who bring the name of Newry and the Carlingford Lough area to a global audience.

People are coming again to visit the Carlingford Lough region in increasing numbers and unlike the past, fewer of its inhabitants are leaving. It seems that there is a revival across the spectrum of life here. Political developments in the '90s have accelerated the pace which has led to improved collective confidence.

Once a small settlement at the head of a strand, Newry now enjoys city status. Although small in physical size, the city of Newry is well positioned to embrace the inevitable challenges and new opportunities. Throughout its history, invaders arriving via Carlingford Lough recognised the potential offered by the entire region and leaders have always attempted to make it a stronghold for their own ends. Nowadays it is the road that links Newry and the surrounding area to the rest of the country. Its geographical location and enterprise of its people was recognised by Nicholas Bagenal in the Middle Ages when he proposed an ambitious but insightful plan to Queen Elizabeth I. The fact that he invested some of his own money to fulfilling those ambitions when the Queen dismissed the plan tells us a lot about his belief in the dream – that Newry and Carlingford Lough could and would be a major feature in the trading and cultural life of Europe.

Acknowledgements

This book has been brought about by the contributions of many people. In particular, we would like to acknowledge the generosity of the following individuals who allowed us to harvest the details and anecdotes which they had grown over months and years of research and experience. They – like so many of us who feel deeply connected to the place we live in – were keen to share their knowledge and insights so that this window into this part of the world is opened as widely as possible.

John Allen, Greencastle.

Liam Bradley, local historian

Mark Brennan, Killowen Historical Society

David Cooper, The Boating Club, Rostrevor

Noreen Cunningham, Curator, Newry and Mourne Museum

Michael Durkin, writer and local historian

Mary Goss, Newry Feis Committee, local historian

Robert Linden, local historian.

Matthew McGrath, Viking historian, Kilbroney Conservation Centre, Rostrevor

Sean Patterson, local maritime historian

Elizabeth Rice, Producer, Your Place and Mine, BBC

Colum Sands, singer and songwriter

Gerry Sloan, The Boating Club, Rostrevor

Paddy Small, local historian

Sincere thanks to you all.
Marie & Colum

Dear Reader

This book is from our much complimented illustrated book series which includes:-

Belfast	Drogheda & the Boyne Valley
By the Lough's North Shore	Blanchardstown, Castleknock and the Park
East Belfast	Dundrum, Stillorgan & Rathfarnham
South Belfast	Blackrock, Dún Laoghaire, Dalkey
Antrim, Town & Country	Bray and North Wicklow
Inishowen	Limerick's Glory
Donegal Highlands	Galway on the Bay
Donegal, South of the Gap	Connemara
Donegal Islands	The Book of Clare
Sligo	Armagh
Mayo	Ring of Gullion
Fermanagh	Carlingford Lough
Omagh	The Mournes
Cookstown	Heart of Down
Dundalk & North Louth	Strangford Shores

For the more athletically minded our illustrated walking book series includes:-

Bernard Davey's Mourne   Tony McAuley's Glens
Bernard Davey's Mourne Part 2

And from our Music series:-

Colum Sands, Between the Earth and the Sky

We can also supply prints, individually signed by the artist, of the paintings featured in the above titles as well as many other areas of Ireland.

For details on these superb publications and to view samples of the paintings they contain, you can visit our web site at **www.cottage-publications.com** or alternatively you can contact us as follows:-

Telephone: +44 (028) 9188 8033   Fax: +44 (028) 9188 8063

Cottage
Publications

Cottage Publications
is an imprint of
Laurel Cottage Ltd
15 Ballyhay Road
Donaghadee, Co. Down
N. Ireland, BT21 0NG